Marinus Willett

Saviour of The Mohawk Valley

By AJ Berry & James F. Morrison

Joyce gave this book to me 11-21-14 for my 90th birthday. She was very sick but came to my party.

Books by AJ Berry & James F. Morrison
Revolutionary War Pension Series
Non-Fiction
Don't Shoot, Part 1
Don't Shoot, Part 2
Don't Shoot, Part 3
Don't Shoot, Part 4
Don't Shoot, Part 5
Don't Shoot, Part 6
Don't Shoot, Part 7
The Colonels of Tryon County
SHORTS
Fort Plain & Fort Plank
Cherry Valley Massacre November 11, 1778
Raids on The Canajoharry 1780
Colonel Jacob Klock
Colonel Jacob Klock & The Palatine District
The Battle of Johnstown

Books by AJ Berry
Non-Fiction
Times Past
Pieter. My Precious Hyper-Active Son
It Is NOT Luck!
Favorites from The Pensions.
Gitty, The Little Slave Girl

The PHOTO Books
Memories of St. Johnsville (Black print and or color)
Memories of Fort Plain (Black print and or color)
Out and About The Mohawk Valley (Black print or color)
Rufus Grider in Color
St. Johnsville Fire Department

The Terror Series
Non-Fiction
A Time of Terror
So It Was Written
Brothers in Arms

Out of Time Series
Historical Fiction
Out of Time

In Her Time
Time for Healing
The Time Traveler's Children
The Time Traveler's Husband
Into The Time Slip
Stuck In Time
Twist In Time
Time for Love
Papa's Time
Time to Tell Mama
As Time Passes
Never Enough Time
Layers of Time
Time and More Time

Counting Series
Historical Fiction
One for The Money
Two for The Show
Three to Make Ready
Four to Go
Five for The Fire

The Browns' Children
Historical Fiction
The Tail That Wagged The Dog
Where Have All The Crickets Gone?

Opie Series
All About the Palatines
Historical Fiction
In The Beginning
The Leaving
Tar Camps
Into The Valley

Copyright 2014
AJ Berry

Foreward

Reminder, since none of us were alive during this time, of course, one must rely upon the information passed down through the generations. The book is compiled by AJ Berry and James F. Morrison, and it consists of stories and documents concerning Marinus Willett. He was an able and capable commander and had a good rapport with the inhabitants of the Mohawk Valley. Willett was a natural commander of men and was greatly respected.

Some of the reports are similar and yet have different details. We leave it to you to ferret out what interests you. To make the book easier to read, paragraphs were added.

In his earlier years, Willett was known as a rabble rouser and often waded into dangerous situations. He is described as a large man and a bit rough around the edges.

The early records of the New York City's Sons of Liberty list him as a member. Those records indicate that he was a front line (street) leader like Isaac Sears and John Scott. Willett, backed by other Sons of Liberty members, seized arms from the British while trying to evacuate their arsenal from the city. This act of bravery, being completely unarmed, seizing the reins of the wagon's horse, astonished both the escorting British soldiers and witnesses. Later, these muskets were used to arm the New York troops raised in 1775.

The first part of the Willett book mostly is about his life in the valley, and the focus is on that part of his life. There are some unpublished letters and documents in the book, which James F. Morrison has generously shared. Jim is the historian and researcher, as always and he does careful and meticulous work which can be trusted.

THE SURVIVING SECRETARY
MADE BY MARINUS WILLETT

The description of Marinus Willett's early existence is scant, he was a cabinet maker by trade in New York City and apparently always interested in the political scene.

On June 28th, 1775 Willett received a commission as a Captain of the Second Company in Colonel Alexander McDougall's First New York Regiment. Marinus was 35 years old at that time. He participated in the Canadian campaign, and was placed in command of Fort St. John during its American occupation.

Included in this book is Willett's widow's application for Bounty Land. He was married 3 times. On a personal note, Margaret was his last wife, and she succeeded him. Willett's first wife of 33 years, Mary Pearsee, died at Cedar Grove in 1793. He lost no time in becoming enamored of Susannah Vardill, a beautiful widow who had already buried two husbands. She was described as "the reigning toast of New York society." They were married on October 3, 1793, three months to the day after his first wife's death. The marriage became an unhappy one. Willett discovered that he had gotten more than he bargained for because his new wife turned out to be a vixen and a spitfire. Susannah loved to gossip--even about her husband; and the marriage eventually soured. Mrs. Willett filed for divorce in 1799. From reports it appears that Willett was very grateful. In that time, divorce was not easy to obtain, and so the reasons must have been easily proven.

Marinus Willett soon lost his heart to Margaret Bancker, the young daughter of Willett's friends, Christopher and Mary Smith Bancker. Willett was 59; she was 24. Despite the disparity in their ages, they married. This third marriage for Willett produced four children--three sons and a daughter. One son became a physician, another a minister, and the third a lawyer.

An ardent foe of Alexander Hamilton and the Federalists, he cast his lot with the anti-Federalists, joining Gov. George Clinton and Aaron Burr in unsuccessfully opposing New York's ratification of the new national constitution.

Willett was elected to the New York State Assembly in 1784 but resigned to become sheriff of the City and County of New York.

In 1807, he was appointed Mayor of New York City to succeed DeWitt Clinton, and served until 1808. [For the first 150 years of the city's existence, mayors were appointed.] Four years later, Clinton defeated Willett for the post of lieutenant governor.

The object of this book is to tell the story about Willett's time in the Mohawk Valley, and not about his life before or after. Keep in mind that Marinus Willett never ran from danger or the enemy, he searched out the enemy and took appropriate action, side by side with his men. In turn, his men respected him and followed him. The Mohawk Valley never forgot the man who did so much hands-on service to the area.

The book, Colonel Marinus Willett, The Hero of Mohawk Valley is included in the back of this book and it is a gem. The sons of the Colonel were able to give the author many interesting insights into the Colonel. It is out of copyright and is now public domain, able to be used by others.

I took the liberty of breaking up the extremely long paragraphs and making smaller paragraphs so the modern reader will be more comfortable. AJ Berry

The following is a description of Marinus Willett's military rank from James F. Morrison.

Willett's title of rank was Lieutenant Colonel Commandant of the 5th NY until it was consolidated with the Second NY on January 1, 1781. Willett was no longer part of the Continental Army. He was appointed Lieutenant Colonel Commandant of the Levies on April 27, 1781 and the militia was to co-operate with him. Seniority in rank was an issue with Continental officers when they were in the valley, such as when Lieutenant Colonel Commandant George Reid was sent to the Mohawk Valley in late 1781 and early 1782. Reid considered himself to be in command of the Mohawk Valley. The same when Colonel Philip Van Cortlandt was at Fort Schuyler and Forts Herkimer and Dayton in early 1781 until they marched in July to join Washington's Army. Van Cortlandt was a full colonel in the Continental Army, and he out ranked Willett. – James F. Morrison.

Marinus Willett--July 31, 1740 – August 22, 1830.

Painting on front cover by Ralph Earl, 1791.

Table of Contents

M. Willett Lt Col

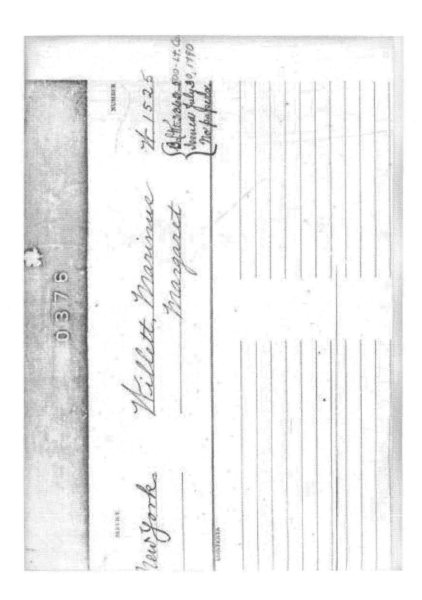

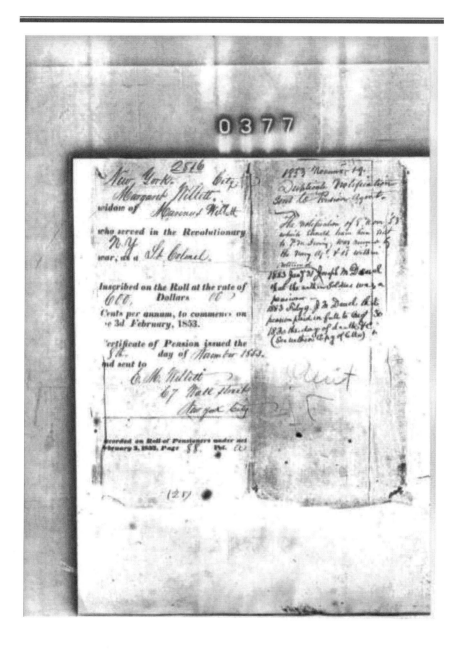

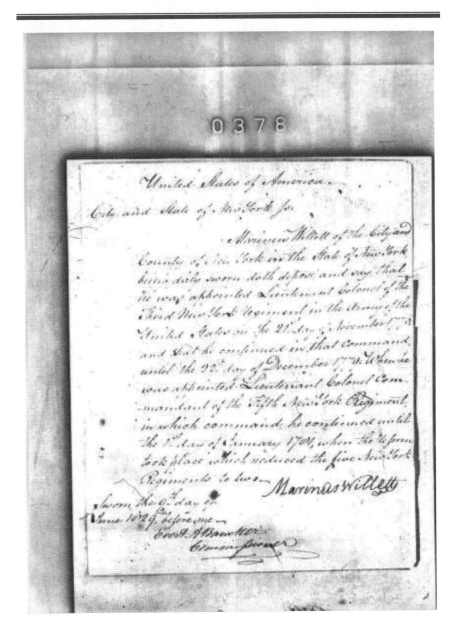

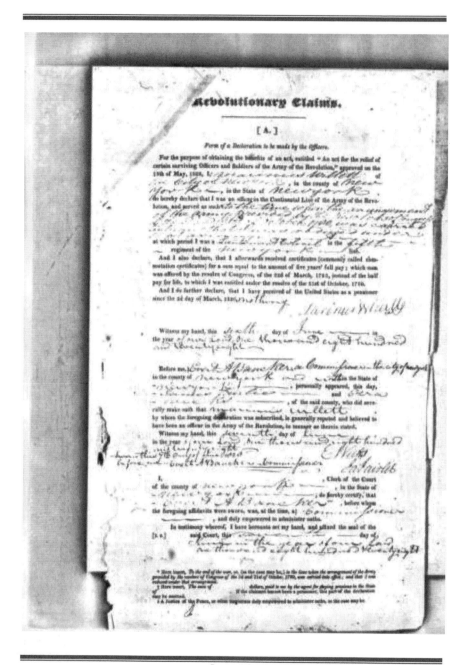

Colonel Willett appeared in the Mohawk Valley early in the war, before he came to command in 1781. The following is from A Time of Terror. 2005, by AJ Berry.

The Battle of Oriskany

General Nicholas Herkimer led his army on into battle. If he had been cautious before, now he was bold. His planned course lay on the south side of the river where for three or four miles, hills rose up from valleys with occasional gullies. The trickling springs and the spring freshets had cut more than one ravine where even in the summer the water still moistened the earth. Corduroy roads had been constructed over the some of the marshes. Herkimer had to cross a deep crooked S-shaped ravine with a marshy bottom, which was spanned, by a causeway and bridge of logs. Sir John Johnson covered this spot with marksmen, leaving an **INLET** for the entrance of the Americans but no **OUTLET** for their escape. He placed his best troops on the road westward where real fighting had to be done. It was a trap waiting to be sprung and Herkimer and his men were entering the trap.

The soldiers hurried on, not in a soldierly order, not watching against the enemy, the eight hundred men marched on oblivious to their danger. They reached the ravine at ten in the morning. The advance guard had reached the higher ground. Then the woods became alive and exploded with violence.

The one break in the whole wretched affair was that the Indians violated their promise to hold back shooting until the signal was given. They showed themselves a few moments too soon, so that Herkimer's rearguard was shut out of the trap instead of in and had a chance to flee.

The rearguard ran for their lives but in many cases they were outrun by the Indians and suffered almost as severely as their comrades whom they had abandoned. Then the butchery started. The men who had taunted Herkimer and called him a coward were the first to fall, just as Herkimer had predicted.

Most of Herkimer's troops were untested by battle; they were strong from their labors in the fields, but not strong with experience. Some had fought in the French and Indians Wars and learned about battle, but many were young and had never faced the enemy before. The confidence the young men felt was soon shattered, the battle was the bloodiest of the war.

Heaven interposed at the height of battle and sent down a terrible thunder shower which stopped the slaughter. In that day of flintlocks and using live fire, firing amid torrents of rain was not possible. Except for the fortunate thunderstorm, the battle would have been lost.

This gave the Americans time to recover their senses. Herkimer, very early in the action was desperately wounded in the leg by a shot, which killed his horse. He had his saddle placed at the foot of a beech tree and sitting on it, propped himself against the trunk. He calmly lit his pipe and continued to give orders, which saved many of his men. The calm that Herkimer presented in the midst of battle gave the men courage.

Previous to the battle at Fort Stanwix, the British sent for the Indians (Senecas) to come and see them whip the rebels; and at the same time they stated that they did not wish to have them fight, but wanted to have them just sit down, smoke their pipes and look on. The potential for quick scalpings pleased the Indians. The British told the Indians it would be over very soon and not be much of a fight.

The Indians went but instead of smoking and looking on they had to fight for their lives. Losses were high among the Indians, and they were not pleased with the outcome. Their mourning was excessive and was expressed by yells, shrieks, howlings and gesticulations.

Quick scalpings did not happen though some were taken; St. Leger offered $20 for each American scalp taken at the battle. The usual bounty was eight dollars except those of officers and committeemen, which brought $10 to $20.

When the shower was about over, Sir John Johnson seeing that the Indians were yielding, sent back to camp for a reinforcement of his "Royal Yorkers," under his brother-in-law, Captain Stephen Watts. These troops disguised themselves like Mohawk Valley Militia by turning their coats inside out, but were quickly recognized by the Americans. At once to the fury of battle was added the bitterness of mutual hate, spite and vengeance.

If the previous fighting had been murderous the next phase was even worse. Firearms were thrown aside, the two forces mingled, they grasped each other by the clothes, and hair, slashed and stabbed with their hunting knives, thrust with bayonets.

Herkimer's army suffered a tactical disaster. This was converted into a triumph due to the calm, common sense command of Herkimer. According to his plan the advance and attack of his column of Mohawk Valley men was to be a combined movement involving a simultaneous sortie from Fort Stanwix.

Once the storm abated, the Americans were placed two and three to a tree so that while one would be shooting, another would be loading his musket.

The planned sortie from Fort Stanwix was not made in time to save Herkimer's life. In addition the Militia suffered the loss of over two-thirds of the men in those killed, wounded or taken prisoner. It is too bad the scouts could not have reached the fort in time to bring reinforcements.

Colonel Marinus Willett took advantage of the thunderstorm to make his sortie from the fort and attack the encampment of the Indians and Loyalists.

St. Leger had three batteries; the first-three light guns; the second-four small mortars; the third-three more small guns. All these guns were totally inadequate for siege purposes, whereas there were fourteen pieces of artillery mounted in the fort. St. Leger had two six-pounders, but the carriages were found to be so rotten that they had to be reconstructed on the spot, and consequently could not have been of service when they were most needed. The redoubts to cover the British batteries, St. Leger's line of approaches and his encampment were all on the north side of the fort. These were occupied by 250 to 350 Regulars and Provincials. Sir John Johnson's camp or works, held by about 133 Loyalist troops, were to the southward.

It was against the latter that Willett made his sortie. St. Leger's men and those of Sir John Johnson were widely separated and independent of each other. They were supposed to be patrolled by the Indians but during the sortie the Indians were all away assaulting Herkimer and the encampment was largely left unprotected.

Willett's sortie was without peril. He had plenty of time to plunder Sir John Johnson's camp and three times send out seven wagons, loaded them, and sent them back into the post without the loss of a man is proof that he met with no opposition.

When he realized what was happening, Sir John Johnson had to hurry back his Royal Yorkers from the battleground. He left with the hope that the completion of the bloody work on the battlefield would be performed by the Indians.

But the Indians had their fill of fighting which was fortunate for the survivors of Herkimer's column. Oriskany belonged to the men of the Mohawk Valley although they were completely trapped, they defended themselves with desperation for five or six hours and displayed great courage under fire.

The slaughter at Oriskany was terrible. St. Leger claimed that 400 of Herkimer's men were killed and 200 captured, leaving only 200 to escape. No such number of prisoners was ever accounted for.

The Americans admitted 200 were killed, one fourth of the whole army. St. Leger placed the number of Indians killed at 30, and the like number wounded, including some favorite chiefs and warriors. The Senecas alone lost 36 killed, and in all the tribes twice as many must have been killed.

Butler mentions New Yorkers (Johnson's Yorkers) killed, Captain McDonald; Captain Watts dangerously wounded and one subaltern. (Subaltern, is an officer holding a military rank just below that of Captain.) Of the Tory Rangers, Captains James Wilson and Henry Hare were killed. The death list of Privates must have been high.

The loss of British and Indians must have approached about 150 killed. Eyewitnesses estimated the loss of the enemy as great as that of the Americans. Because of poor record keeping the real toll will never be known.

Most commanders from the war claimed the enemy losses greater than they were and their losses much less than they were. The same story went for the number of men engaged in battle. If there was a defeat, the commander overestimated the amount of men the enemy had facing them. It was a way of covering themselves with more glory than they were entitled to claim. Who could prove otherwise?

The Patriot dead included Colonel Ebenezer Cox who was one of the first to fall and the most vocal of Herkimer's taunters. Majors John Eisenlord, Nicholas Van Slyck; Augustinus Klapsattle and Captains Henry Diefendorf, Robert Crouse, Peter Bowman, Andrew Dillenback, John Davis, Samuel Pettingill, and Christopher P. Fox fell with no less than four members of the Tryon County Committee of Safety, who were present as volunteers.

The Committee of Safety members were Samuel Billington, John Dygert and Jacob Snell. Thomas Spencer, the Oneida, who gave the warning to the Patriots, was also among the killed. Isaac Paris was captured and then tortured and killed after the battle. The heads of the Patriot organization in the valley were swept off. In no other battle of the Revolution did the deaths rise so high.

Frightful barbarities were wreaked on the bodies of the dead and on the prisoners who fell into the hands of the Indians. The

Patriots were able to carry off their wounded. Herkimer was taken on a litter of boughs to the river and then down the river to his home.

Shortly after the amputation of his leg, he died from blood loss on the seventeenth of August.

When General Arnold and his troops reached Oriskany days later, the stench was so great from the hundreds of rotting bodies that they could not bury their heroic countrymen, and their bones were left on the ground to be bleached by the sun. The stench of death lasted for many months over the battlefield.

The tears flowed for a long time in the valley.

Source Material:

The Centennial Celebrations of the State of New York
Prepared pursuant to a Concurrent Resolution
of the Legislature of 1878 and Chapter 391 of the Laws of 1879
By Allen C. Beach, Secretary of State. Albany
Weed, Parsons & Co. Printers 1879.

The Orderly Book of Sir John Johnson
During the Oriskany Campaign
1776-1777 Annotated by Wm. L. Stone
Albany Joel Munsell, 1882

The Sortie of Colonel Willett
or Colonel Willett "Sallies Forth"

The British abandoned Fort Stanwix in 1768 and when they returned in 1777 they expected to find a tumble down fort. Instead they discovered it had been rebuilt as a log and earthen fortress. It was not quite completed when the British arrived in August, but it was good enough to use for the purpose of defending the valley. The fort was renamed Fort Schuyler after General Philip Schuyler and was defended by about 750 troops, another surprise which was waiting for the British and Loyalist troops.

Brigadier-General (Lt. Col.) Barry St. Leger had over 700 trained troops. All told, the army of St. Leger consisted of seventeen hundred men, Indians included. Captain Joseph Brant commanded the Indians. Besides this, St. Leger had only a few light pieces, barely enough to harass much less to destroy the fort. They appeared at the fort on August 2, 1777. In any war they waged in America, supplies were a problem and transporting them to the field of battle, still a bigger problem. Almost all supplies were brought from England by ship.

Colonel Peter Gansevoort (age 28) was commander at Fort Schuyler with the second in command, Lt. Colonel Marinus Willett (age 37).

St. Leger presented an offer of surrender to the fort on August 3, 1777 but Gansevoort ignored the offer. There was not much St. Leger's men could do against the fortified walls, all they could do was hope to starve out the men and pick them off one by one as the opportunity presented itself.

When General Nicholas Herkimer left Fort Dayton on August 4 and started the march to the fort, he did not know the enemy had advance warning of his approach with the Militia. Sir William Johnson's Indian wife Molly Brant saw the troops collecting and sent a message to her brother, Captain Joseph Brant. The enemy's plan was to finish off the Militia fast and end the insurrection.

Herkimer sent a message to Gansevoort that he was on the way and he wanted to coordinate an attack by the Militia with an attack from the troops in the fort. The signal for attack would be three cannon shots from the fort, a signal that could be heard for miles through the wilderness.

The messengers did not arrive and the signal was not given. Colonel Ebenezer Cox and several other officers urged an immediate advance. In their eagerness to attack, several told Herkimer that "some of your near relatives are in the camp of the enemy, and you ought to be there too". Some went so far as to call him a coward to his face. In vain he urged them to wait for the signal from the fort. At last Herkimer said: "March on, a few hours will tell us which are the brave!"

The Loyalists and the Indians watched the progress of the army coming towards them, into an ambush. Suddenly the guns erupted and the bloody battle began. During the Battle of Oriskany, (two miles from Fort Schuyler) further preparations were being made at Fort Schuyler. Lt. Col. Willett was given the task of raiding the Loyalist and Indian encampments.

The battle was a ferocious one and Colonel Cox was among the first to die. During the battle a sudden thunderstorm stopped the fighting for a short time. As soon as the storm was over, the battle resumed and at this point, the official record said Willett "sallied forth". Willett and 250 men raided the enemy camps, those of the Indians and Loyalists. The British and Indian encampments were left with just a few men to defend it during the battle on August 6, 1777. The Indians were supposed to be guarding the encampments.

The raid was a total success, both of the encampments were destroyed. In addition the raiders took food provisions, 50 brass kettles and more than 100 blankets (two articles which were much needed), a quantity of muskets, tomahawks, spears, ammunition, clothing, deerskins, Indian clothing, personal papers, correspondence and Sir John Johnson's personal orderly book. There was time for Willett to plunder three times and to send seven loaded wagons back to the fort without the loss of a man.

The Indians usually fought naked; and when they returned to their encampment they discovered they were left without clothing or blankets. This did not make them happy at all and they began to complain loudly. They suffered a high loss of lives from the battle. Indians were better scouts and runners and not frontal attack warriors. The loud wailing from the Indians mourning their friends was very loud through the encampment.

Though they left the field sure they had lost, the Mohawk Valley men knocked the fight out of the Indians and stopped the advance of the enemy into the valley. They fought ferociously when surrounded and turned a disaster into a success.

When the news of a large force of men under General Benedict Arnold was coming west to lift the siege, St. Leger knew it was time to leave. Really he was left with no choice, the Indians left in great haste and the white troops were left alone.

On the 23rd of August the British and Loyalists hastily left the scene; abandoning tents, guns and stores and retreated. The siege and the battle became history.

Many mistakes were made on both sides during the war. It has been said "Victory went to the side making the fewest mistakes."

Source Material:

The Frontiersmen of New York
by Jeptha R. Simms
Albany, NY 1883

The Orderly Book of Sir John Johnson During the Oriskany

Campaign 1776-1777
Annotated by Wm. L. Stone
With an Historical Introduction illustrating the Life of Johnson by
J. Watts De Peyster, and Some Tracings from the Foot-Prints of
the Tories, or Loyalists in America by T. R. Myers. Albany, Joel
Munsell, 1882

The Centennial Celebrations of the State of New York
By Allen C. Beach, Secretary of State.
Albany Weed, Parsons & Co. Printers 1879.

By 1781, the situation in the Mohawk Valley was desperate.

The Story of Old Fort Plain and the Middle Mohawk Valley
by Nelson Greene
O'Connor Brothers Publishers, Fort Plain, NY 1915

CHAPTER XIX.

Of the conditions in the Mohawk country at the opening of 1781, Beer's History of Montgomery County has the following:

"Gloomy indeed was the prospect at this time in the Mohawk valley. Desolation and destitution were on every side. Of an abundant harvest almost nothing remained. The Cherry Valley, Harpersfield, and all other settlements toward the headwaters of the Susquehanna, had been entirely deserted for localities of greater safety. Some idea of the lamentable condition of other communities in Tryon county may be obtained from a statement addressed to the legislature, December 20, 1780, by the supervisors of the county. In that document it was estimated that 700 buildings had been burned in the county; 613 persons had deserted to the enemy; 354 families had abandoned their dwellings; 197 lives had been lost; 121 persons had been carried into captivity, and hundreds of farms lay uncultivated by reason of the enemy.

"Nor were the terrible sufferings indicated by these statistics, mitigated by a brighter prospect. Before the winter was past, Brant was again hovering about with predatory bands to destroy what little property remained. Since the Oneidas had been driven from their country, the path of the enemy into the valley was almost unobstructed.

It was with difficulty that supplies could be conveyed to Forts Plain and Dayton without being captured, and transportation to Fort Schuyler was of course far more hazardous. The militia had been greatly diminished and the people dispirited by repeated invasions, and the destruction of their property; and yet what information could be obtained indicated that another incursion might be looked for to sweep perhaps the whole extent of the valley, contemporaneously with a movement from the north toward Albany. Fort Schuyler was so much injured by flood and fire in the spring of 1781, that it was abandoned, the garrison retiring to the lower posts; and all the upper part of the valley was left open to the savages. [The Fort Schuyler troops went to Forts Dayton, Herkimer and Fort Plain.]

"Gov. Clinton was greatly pained by the gloomy outlook and knowing that Col. Willett was exceedingly popular in the valley, earnestly solicited his services in this quarter. Willett had just been appointed to the command of one of the two new regiments formed by the consolidation of the remnants of five New York regiments, and it was with reluctance that he left the main army for so difficult and harassing an undertaking as the defense of the Mohawk region.

The spirit of the people, at this time lower than at any other during the long struggle, began to revive when Col. Willett appeared among them. It was in June that he repaired to Tryon county to take charge of the militia levies and state troops that he might be able to collect. In the letter to Gov. Clinton making known the weakness of his command.

Col. Willett said: "I confess myself not a little disappointed in having such a trifling force for such extensive business as I have on my hands; and also that nothing is done to enable me to avail myself of the militia. The prospect of a suffering county hurts me. Upon my own account I am not uneasy. Everything I can do shall be done, and more cannot be looked for. If it is, the reflection that I have done my duty must fix my own tranquility."

Willett made his headquarters at Fort Plain, which continued to be the valley headquarters during the rest of the war. He had not been long at Fort Plain before his soldierly qualities and great ability as a commander were brought into play. Willett came to his valley headquarters in June and, in a month's time, occurred the first raid he had to combat-that led by Dockstader.

The following is largely written from Simms's account of the Currytown Invasion and Sharon Springs battle:

1781, July 9, 500 Indians and Tories entered the town of Root on one of the raids that devastated Montgomery county the latter years of the war. Their commander was Capt. John Dockstader, a Tory who had gone from the Mohawk country to Canada. The settlement of Currytown (named after William Corry, the patentee of the lands thereabout) was the first objective of these marauders. Here a small block-house had been erected, near the dwelling of Henry Lewis, and surrounded with a palisade. At about ten in the morning the enemy entered the settlement. Jacob Dievendorf, a pioneer settler, was at work in the field with his two sons, Frederick and Jacob and a negro boy named Jacobus Blood. The last two were captured and Frederick, a boy of 14, ran toward the fort but was overtaken, tomahawked and scalped. Mrs. Dievendorf, in spite of being a fleshy woman, made for the fort with several girl children and half a dozen slaves and reached it In safety, on the way breaking down a fence by her weight in climbing over.

Peter Bellinger, a brother of Mrs. Dievendorf, was plowing and hearing the alarm, unhitched a plow horse and, mounting it, rode for the Mohawk and escaped although pursued by several Indians. Rudolf Keller and his wife happened to be at the fort, when the enemy appeared; Keller, Henry Lewis and Conrad Enders being the only men in the blockhouse at that time.

Frederick Lewis and Henry Lewis jr. were the first to reach the fort after the invaders' appearance. Frederick Lewis fired three successive guns to warn the settlers of danger and several, taking the warning, escaped safely to the forest. Philip Bellinger thus escaped but was severely wounded and died with friends shortly after. Rudolf Keller's oldest son, seeing the enemy approach, ran home and hurried the rest of the family to the woods, the Indians entering the Keller house just as the fugitives disappeared into the forest. Jacob Tanner and his family were among the last to reach the blockhouse On seeing the Indians corning, Tanner fled from his house, with his gun in one hand and a small child in his other arm, followed by his wife with an infant in her arms and several children running by her side holding onto her skirts. Several redmen with uplifted tomahawks chased the Tanner family toward the fort. Finding that they could not overtake them, one of the Indians fired at Tanner, the ball passing just over the child's head he carried and entering a picket of the fort. The defenders fired several shots at the savages and the fleeing family entered the blockhouse safely.

The Indians plundered and burned all the buildings in the settlement, a dozen or more, except the house of David Lewis. Lewis was a Tory and, although his house was set on fire, an Indian chief, with whom he was acquainted, gave him permission to put it out when they were gone. Jacob Moyer and his father, who were cutting timber in the woods not far from Yates, were found dead and scalped, one at each end of the log. They were killed by the party who pursued Peter Bellinger.

The lad, Frederick Dievendorf, after lying insensible for several hours, recovered and crawled toward the fort. He was seen by his uncle, Keller, who went out to meet him. As he approached, the lad, whose clothes were dyed in his own blood, still bewildered, raised his hands Imploringly and besought his uncle not to kill him. Keller took him up in his arms and carried him to the fort. His wounds were properly dressed and he recovered, but was killed several years after by a falling tree. Jacob Dievendorf senior, fled before the Indians, on their approach and, in his flight, ran past a prisoner named James Butterfield, and at a little distance farther on hid himself under a fallen tree. His pursuers enquired of Butterfleld what direction he had taken. "That way," said the prisoner, pointing in a different direction. Although several Indians passed by the fallen tree Dievendorf remained undiscovered.

An old man named Putman, captured at this time, was too infirm to keep up with the enemy and was killed and scalped not far from his home.

The Currytown captives taken along by the enemy were Jacob Dievendorf jr., the Negro Jacob, Christian and Andrew Bellinger, sons of Frederick Bellinger, and a little girl named Miller, ten or twelve years old. Christian Bellinger had been in the nine month [militia] service. He was captured on going to get a span of horses, at which time he heard an alarm gun fired at Fort Plain. The horses were hobbled together and the Indians, with a bark rope, had tied the hobble to a tree in a favorable place to capture the one who came for them, who chanced to be young Bellinger. His brother (Andrew) was taken so young and kept so long-to the end of the war- and was so pleased with Indian life, that Christian had to go a third time to get him to return with him. Michael Stowitts (son of Philip G. P. Stowitts, who was killed on the patriot side In the Oriskany battle) was made a prisoner on the Stowitts farm, and is credited with having given the invaders an exaggerated account of the strength defending the fort, which possibly prevented its capture; but it is well known that even small defenses were avoided by the enemy, who did not like exposure to certain death.

On the morning of the same day of the Currytown raid (1781, July 9) Col. Willett sent out, from Fort Plain, Capt. Lawrence Gros with a scouting party of 40 men. Their mission had the double object of scouting for the enemy and provisions. Knowing that the settlements of New Dorlach and New Rhinebeck were inhabited mostly by Tories and that he might get a few supplies there, Gros led his men in that direction. Near the former home of one Baxter, he struck the trail of the enemy and estimated their number from their footprints at 600 men at least. Gros sent two scouts to follow the enemy and then marched his squad to Bowman's (Canajoharie) creek to await their report. The scouts came upon the enemy's camp of the night before after going about a mile. A few Indians were seen cooking food at the fires-making preparations, as the Americans supposed, for the return of their comrades who had gone to destroy Currytown. The two rangers returned quickly to Gros and reported their find, and the captain dispatched John Young and another man, both mounted, on a gallop to Fort Plain to inform Col. Willett.

The commandant sent a messenger to Lieut. Col. Vedder, at Fort Paris, with orders to collect all troops possible, at his post and elsewhere, and to make a rapid march to the enemy's camp. Col. Willett detailed all the garrison of Fort Plain he could, with safety detach from that post, for the field. In addition he collected what militia he could from the neighborhood and set out. Passing Fort Clyde in Freysbush, Willett drafted into his ranks what men could there be spared and about midnight he joined Capt. Gros at Bowman's creek.

The American force numbered 260 men, many of whom were militia. Col. Willett's battalion set out and, at daybreak, reached the enemy's camp, which was in a cedar swamp on the north side of the western turnpike, near the center of the present town of Sharon and about two miles east of Sharon Springs. This camp was on the highest ground of the swamp, only a few rods from the turnpike. On the south side of the road, a ridge of land may be seen and still south of that a small valley. By a roundabout march, Willett reached this little dale and there drew up his force in a half-circle formation. The men were instructed to take trees or fallen logs and not to leave them and to reserve their fire until they had a fair shot.

The enemy was double the number of the patriot force and stratagem was resorted to by the Fort Plain commandant. He sent several men over the ridge to show themselves, fire upon the raiders and then flee, drawing the foe toward the American ranks. This ruse completely succeeded and the entire Tory and Indian band snatched up their weapons and chased the American skirmishers who fled toward Willett's ambuscade, Frederick

Bellinger being overtaken and killed. The enemy was greeted with a deadly fire from the hidden soldiers and a fierce tree to tree fight began which lasted for two hours until the Tories and Indians, badly punished, broke and fled. John Strobeck, who was a private in Captain Gros's company and in the hottest part of the fight, said afterwards that "the Indians got tired of us and made off." Strobeck was wounded in the hip.

During the battle, from a basswood stump, several shots were fired with telling effect at the patriots. William H. Seeber rested his rifle on the shoulder of Henry Failing and gave the hollow stump a centre shot, after which fire from that quarter ceased. About this time, it is said, the enemy were recovering from their first panic, learning they so greatly outnumbered the Continental force.

A story is told that Col. Willett, seeing the foe gaining confidence shouted in a loud voice, "My men, stand your ground and I'll bring up the levies and we'll surround the damned rascals!"

The enemy hearing this, and expecting to be captured or slain by an increased American body, turned and ran. In the pursuit Seeber and Failing reached the stump the former had hit and found it was hollow. Seeing a pool of blood on the ground, Col. Willett observed: "One that stood behind that stump will never get back to Canada."

The enemy, in their retreat, were hotly pursued by the Americans, led by Col. Willett in person and so complete was the defeat of the raiders that Willett's men captured most of their camp equipage and plunder obtained the day before in the Currytown raid. Most of the cattle and horses the raiders had taken found their way back to that settlement.

Col. Willett continued the pursuit but a short distance, fearing that he might himself fall into a snare similar to the one he had so successfully set for the enemy. The American force returned victorious to Fort Plain, immediately after the battle, bearing with them their wounded. Their loss of five killed and about the same number wounded was small and due to their protected position and the surprise they sprang on their foe.

The Indians, in their retreat from Sharon, crossed the west creek in New Dorlach (near the former Col. Rice residence) and made for the Susquehanna. The loss of the enemy was very severe-about 50 killed and wounded-and Dockstader is said to have returned to Canada (after one other engagement) with his force "greatly reduced." Two of the enemy carried a wounded comrade, on a blanket between two poles, all the way to the Genesee valley, where he died.

Five of Willett's men were killed, including Capt. McKean, a brave and efficient officer. He was taken to Van Alstine's fortified house at Canajoharie, which was on the then road from New Dorlach to Fort Plain, and died there the following day, after which he was buried in "soldier's ground" at Fort Plain; which was probably the burial plot about one hundred yards west of that post, remains of which are still to be seen. On the completion of the blockhouse, McKean's body was reburied on the brink of the hill in front of this fortification with military honors.

Among the wounded was a son of Capt. McKean, who was shot in the mouth. Jacob Radnour received a bullet In his right thigh which he carried to his grave. Like that Sir "William Johnson got at Lake George, it gradually settled several inches and made him very lame. Hon. Garrett Dunckel was wounded In the head, "a ball passing in at the right eye and coming out back of the ear." Nicholas Yerdon was wounded in the right wrist, which caused the hand to shrivel and become useless. Adam Strobeck's wound in the hip has been mentioned. All three of the latter came from Freysbush and Radnour, Dunckel and Yerdon were in the Oriskany battle, where Radnour and Yerdon were wounded. All these wounded were borne on litters back to Fort Plain and all recovered.

Finding their force defeated and having to abandon their prisoners in the flight, the Indians guarding them tomahawked and scalped all except the Bellinger boys and Butterfield. The killed at this time included a German named Carl Herwagen, who had been captured by the enemy on their return from Currytown to their camp the previous evening.

After the battle was over Lieut. Col. Veeder arrived from Fort Paris with a company of 100 men, mostly from Stone Arabia. He buried the Americans killed in battle and fortunately found and interred the prisoners who were murdered and scalped near the enemy's former camp. The Dievendorf boy, who had been scalped, was found alive half buried among the dead leaves, with which he had covered himself to keep off mosquitoes and flies from his bloody head.

One of Veeder's men, thinking him a wounded Indian, on account of his gory face, leveled his gun to shoot but it was knocked up by a fellow soldier, and the Currytown boy's life was spared for almost four-score years more. Young Dievendorf and the little Miller girl, also found alive, were tenderly taken back to Fort Plain, but the latter died on the way. Doctor Faught, a German physician of Stone Arabia, tended the wounds of both Jacob Dievendorf and his brother Frederick Dievendorf and both recovered. Jacob Dievendorf's scalped head was five years in healing. He became one of the wealthiest farmers of Montgomery county and died Oct. 8, 1859, over seventy-eight years after his terrible experience of being scalped and left for dead by his red captors on the bloody field of Sharon.

The battle of Sharon was fought, almost entirely, by men from the present limits of the town of Minden-the Fort Plain garrison, with additions from that of Fort Clyde, and the Minden militia. Some of the soldiers doubtless came from Forts Willett, "Windecker and Plank. The Fort Paris company, as seen, did not get up in time to fight. The list of the Americans wounded at Sharon would indicate that the greater part of Willett's battalion were local men. Probably the men of the Mohawk formed a large percentage of the valley garrisons of that time. There was then little for the men of the Mohawk to do but to guard and fight and, between times, to till the fields which were not too exposed to the enemy's ravages. A considerable population must have clustered in and about the principal forts for protection.

Col. Marinus Willett, who made his headquarters at Fort Plain for the last three years of the war and who was connected with so many of the valley military operations and almost all the patriot successes in the valley, deserves mention here. He was a soldier of the highest qualifications, great courage and daring, a clever and fearless woodsman and an intrepid fighter in the open field. His quick, powerful, decisive blows, such as at Johnstown and Sharon Springs, conspired to end the raids from Canada which had devastated the valley.

Marinus Willett was born in Jamaica, Long Island, in 1740, the youngest of six sons of Edward Willett, a Queens county farmer. In 1758 he joined the army, under Abercrombie, as a lieutenant in Col. Delaney's regiment. Exposure in the wilderness caused a sickness which confined him in Fort Stanwix until the end of the campaign.

Willett early joined the Whigs, in the contest against British aggression. When the British troops in New York were ordered to Boston, after the skirmish at Lexington in 1775, they attempted to carry off a large quantity of spare arms in addition to their own. Willett resolved to prevent it and, although opposed by the mayor and other Whigs, he captured the baggage wagons containing the weapons, etc., and took them back to the city.

These arms were afterwards used by the first regiment raised by the state of New York. He was appointed second captain of a company In McDougal's regiment and accompanied Montgomery's futile expedition against Quebec. He commanded St. John's until 1776. He was appointed lieutenant-colonel in 1777 and commanded Fort Constitution on the Hudson. In May he was ordered to Fort Stanwix, recently named Fort Schuyler, where he did such signal service. He was left in command of that fort where he remained until 1778, when he joined the army under Washington and fought with him at Monmouth.

He accompanied Sullivan in his campaign against the Indians in 1779. Col. Willett was actively engaged in the Mohawk valley in 1780, 1781, 1782, 1783. So he spent at least four or five years in military service in the Mohawk valley. Washington sent him to talk with the Creek Indians in Florida in 1792 and the same year he was appointed a brigadier-general in the army which was intended to act against the northwestern Indians. He declined this appointment, being opposed to the expedition.

Col. Willett was for some time sheriff and In 1807 was elected Mayor of New York city. He was president of the electoral college in 1824 and died in New York August 23, 1830, in the 91st year of his age.

A portrait of Col. Willett hangs, among those of other former mayors, in the City Hall in New York and shows a face of much intelligence, power and forceful initiative. Marinus Willett was one of the men of iron who made the American republic possible. There are few natural leaders and he was one.

Simms says Willett was a "large man." He was a direct descendant of Thomas Willett, who was a man of great ability and influence in the early years of New York province, and who was the first mayor of New York city after the Dutch rule, being appointed by Gov. Nicolls in 1665. Col. Marinus Willett had a natural son by a Fort Plain woman. This son he cared for and educated and later, when the son was a grown man, he returned to his birthplace and lived here and hereabouts for several years.

The following, concerning Willett, is taken from "New York in the Revolution":

"Captain, Major, Lieutenant-Colonel, Colonel and Acting Brigadier Marinus Willett was a gallant officer. He held many commands and his promotion was rapid. In 1775-6 he was captain in Col. Alexander McDougal's regiment, 1st N. Y. Line. On April 27, 1776, the Provincial Congress recommended him to the Continental Congress for major of the same regiment. In November of the same year he was recommended for lieutenant-colonel of the 3d Line [regiment] and in July, 1780, he was made lieutenant-colonel commandant of the 5th regiment of the line. In 1781 as lieutenant-colonel he commanded a regiment of levies [men drafted into military service] and in 1782 was made full colonel of still another regiment of levies.

After the death of General Nicholas Herkimer, Colonel Willett commanded the Tryon County militia as acting brigadier-general." The regiment of levies, which Willett commanded in 1781 and which engaged in the Sharon and Johnstown battles, is mentioned in a later chapter dealing briefly with the Tryon county troops. It numbered 1008 soldiers, was largely composed of Mohawk river men, and probably formed all or part of the valley garrisons of the time when Fort Plain was the military headquarters of this section.

At German Flats, 1781, were several encounters. One of them was marked by great bravery on the part of Captain Solomon Woodworth and a small party of rangers which he organized. He marched from Fort Dayton to the Royal Grant for the purpose of observation. On the way he fell into an Indian ambush. One of the most desperate and bloody skirmishes of the war hereabouts then ensued. Woodworth and a large number of his scouts were slain. This was the same Woodworth who so valiantly defended the Sacandaga blockhouse, as told in a previous chapter. His company assembled at Fort Plain only a few days previous to the fatal action, which took place at Fairfield. Some of his men were recruited from soldiers of the Fort Plain garrison whose time was soon to expire.

In this year also occurred the heroic defense by Christian Schell of his blockhouse home about five miles north of Herkimer village. Sixty Tories and Indians under Donald McDonald, a Tory formerly of Johnstown, attacked the place, most of the people fleeing to Fort Dayton. Schell had eight sons and two of them were captured in the fields while the old man ran safely home and with his other six sons and Mrs. Schell made a successful defense. They captured McDonald wounded. The enemy drew off having 11 killed and 15 wounded. Schell and one of his boys were killed by Indians in his fields a little later.

Early in May, 1781, high water from the Mohawk destroyed a quantity of stores in Fort Schuyler. On May 12 this post was partially destroyed by fire. The soldiers were playing ball a little distance away and pretty much everything was burned except the palisade and the bombproof, which was saved by throwing dirt on it.

This fire has been said to have been of incendiary origin having been started by a soldier of secret Tory sentiments. Samuel Pettit, who was then one of the garrison, in his old age, told Simms that the fire originated from charcoal used to repair arms in the armory. The post was abandoned and the troops marched down the Forts Dayton and Herkimer, which became now the most advanced posts on this frontier. Some of the Fort Schuyler garrison are said to have been removed to Fort Plain. After the abandonment of Fort Schuyler the principal Mohawk valley posts of Tryon county were, in their order from west to east, as follows: Fort Dayton (at present Herkimer), Fort Herkimer (at present German Flats), Fort Plain, Fort Paris (at Stone Arabia), Fort Johnstown, Fort Hunter. Fort Plain's central position probably influenced its selection as the valley American army head-quarters. Simms says that.

In the spring of 1781, Col. Livingston, with his regiment of New York troops marched up the Mohawk valley to Fort Plain. No mention is made of further disposition of the troops, however. Possibly, these may have been part of "the reinforcements lately ordered northward" referred to by Gen. Washington in his letter of

June 5, 1781, to Gov. Clinton. Washington advocated the concentration of these troops on the Hudson and Mohawk rivers."

In the summer of 1781 Col. Willett went with a scouting party from Fort Plain to Fort Herkimer and on his return stopped at the Herkimer house. Here then lived Capt. George Herkimer, brother of the deceased General, who had succeeded to the Fall Hill estate. At this time a small body of Indians was seen in the woods above the house and Mrs. Herkimer went to the front door and stepped up on a seat on the stoop and, with her arm around the northwest post, she blew an alarm for her husband who with several slaves was hoeing corn on the flats near the river.

Col. Willett came to the door and seeing the woman's exposed position shouted, "Woman, For God's sake, come in or you'll be shot!" He seized hold of Mrs. Herkimer's dress and pulled her inside the house and almost the instant she stepped from the seat to the floor a rifle ball entered the post-instead of her head-leaving a hole long visible. It is presumed that Willett's men quickly drove off the enemy as Captain Herkimer was not harmed.

In July, 1781, a party of 12 Indians made a foray In the Palatine district and captured five persons, on the Shults farm two miles north of the Stone Arabia churches. Three sons of John Shults-Henry, William and John junior, a lad named Felder Wolfe and a negro slave called Joseph went to a field to mow, carrying their guns and stacking them on the edge of the field, skirted on one side by thick woods. From this cover the Indians sprang out, secured the firearms, captured the harvesters and took them all prisoners to Canada. Upon the mowers not returning, people from the farm went to the field and found their scythes, but the guns were missing. These were the only evidences that the harvesters had been made prisoners. They remained in Canada until the end of the war.

The Orderly Book of Sir John Johnson
During the Oriskany Campaign
1776-1777
Annotated by Wm. L. Stone
With an Historical Introduction illustrating the Life of Johnson by J. Watts
De Peyster, and Some Tracings from the Foot-Prints of the Tories, or
Loyalists in America by T. R. Myers.
Albany
Joel Munsell, 1882

GEN. MARINUS WILLETT.

MARINUS WILLETT, the author of *Wllett's Narrative*, was born at Jamaica, Long Island, July 31st, (O. S.), 1740, He was the youngest of six sons of Edward Willett, a Queen's county farmer, and of excellent family-a younger branch, indeed, of that of Judge Thomas Jones, so well known as the author of the *History of New York during the Revolutionary War*, recently edited by Edward F. de Lancey, and published under the auspices of the N. Y. His. Soc. Owing to his family becoming much reduced in its circumstances, young Willett came to New York city and served for a time as a constable, which, in those days, was a position fully as dignified as that of sheriff is now.

He early became imbued with a military spirit, and joined the army under Abercrombie as a lieutenant in Col. de Lancey's regiment in 1758. He was in the disastrous battle at Ticonderoga, and accompanied Bradstreet against Fort Frontenac. Exposure in the wilderness injured his health, and he was laid up by sickness at Fort Stanwix until the end of the campaign. Willett espoused the cause of the colonies when the troubles with the mother country first began. When the British troops in the New York garrison were ordered to Boston after the fight at Lexington, they attempted, in addition to their own, to carry off a large quantity of spare arms.

Willett, learning of this, resolved to prevent it; and, though opposed by the mayor and other Tories, he captured the baggage-wagons containing them and brought them back to the city.

These arms were afterward used by the first regiment raised by the state of New York. For this successful attempt to baffle the British, he drew down on him the bitter hatred of all who were opposed to colonial independence; and hence it is a matter of no surprise when, in speaking of him in his *Tory History of New York*, Judge Jones says "he became a principal leader in all mobs in New York prior to the actual commencement of the rebellion." He was appointed second captain of a company in Col. Mc Dougall's regiment and accompanied Montgomery in his Northern expedition against Quebec.

He was placed in command of St. John's, and held that post until January, 1776. In the same year, he was appointed lieutenant colonel; and, at the opening of the campaign of 1777, was placed in command of Fort Constitution on the Hudson. In May of this year, he was ordered to Fort Stanwix, where he performed signal service, as mentioned in the Introduction , and for which he was voted a sword by congress. This vote of congress, unlike the playful amusement in which that body has, until lately, seemed inclined to indulge, viz: of voting monuments to Herkimer, Steuben, Pulaski, and others, and allowing its action to end in a vote merely, was, we are glad to state, carried out , and the sword was sent direct to Col. Willett by John Hancock. This sword, which is owned by the widow of the late Rev. Mr. Willett, has for several months past been in the careful keeping of a jeweller on William street near the New York Custom House.

After the retreat of St. Leger and Johnson, Willett was left in command of Fort Stanwix, and remained there until the summer of 1778, when he joined the army under Washington, arriving in time to participate in the battle of Monmouth. He accompanied Sullivan in his campaign against the Senecas in 1779, and was actively engaged in the Mohawk valley in, 1781 and 1782. In 1783, he was for a little time in command of the northern portion of New York state, having his headquarters at Albany. A MS. letter, now before me, from Willett to Washington, dated "Albany, 30th Jan., 1783," and signed "M. Willett, Col. Commanding," bears on its back the following endorsement also in his handwriting.

"Permit the bearer Thomas Clump (express rider) to pass to headquarters at New Burgh. Should any accident happen to his horse or himself, all magistrates and other friends are humbly requested to afford him such assistance as he may stand in need of, in order that his dispatches may not be delayed. And any necessary expenses which may accrue on this account, I promise to settle.

M. WILLETT, Col. Commanding."

In 1792, he was sent by Washington to treaty with the Creek Indians at the south, and the same year he was appointed a brigadier general in the army intended to act against the northwestern tribes. This appointment, however, he declined, as he was conscientiously opposed to the expedition. He was for some time sheriff of New York city, and was elected its mayor in 1807. He was also chosen one of the electors of president arid vice-president in 1824, and was made president of the Electoral College. He died in New York city at "Cedar Grove" (as his residence in Broome street was called), full of years and honors, Sunday evening, Aug. 23d, 1830, the anniversary of his battle with Major Ross and Walter Butler, in the 91st year of his age.

The funeral of Col. Willett took place on Tuesday, the 24th of August. The coffin was conveyed into the garden in the rear of his dwelling, under an arbor, which in life had been his favorite resort; a gate was thrown open in the rear, so that the number of visitors who were anxious to view his remains might pass through without confusion.

It was estimated that not less than ten thousand persons availed themselves of the opportunity. The procession formed at his residence, the pallbearers being Col. Troup, Col. Fish, Col. Trumbull, Col. A. Ogden, Major General Morton, Major Fairlie, J.

Pintard, Esq., and Mr. Dominick. The bier was attended by the members of the Cincinnati society, the members of the court of errors, the members of the common council, the judges of the different courts, together with an immense concourse of citizens in carriages and on foot, accompanied by a troop of horse and a corps of New York state artillery.

The procession moved to Trinity church, and the remains, after services conducted by Rev. Dr. De Witt, were deposited in Trinity churchyard. During the afternoon ninety minute-guns were fired on the battery, and volleys of musquetery over the grave. I am informed by an old and highly esteemed resident of New York, who at that time lived near Col. Willett in Broome street, that the funeral procession, carriages included, extended nearly the entire distance from Broome street to Trinity church. Indeed, in view of these public and private manifestations of grief which, on his decease, so spontaneously gushed forth, it is a little surprising that the accomplished and genial editor of *Jones's History of New York*, in alluding to Willett's death, could find nothing more to say about him than that in his latter life, after the war was a very respectable one."

The following notice appeared in the *New York Commercial Advertiser*, at that time edited by my father, Col. William L. Stone, who was Col. Willett's warm friend. "The coffin of Col. Willett was made of pieces of wood, collected by himself, many of them from different revolutionary battle fields. The corpse, in compliance with the written request of the deceased, was habited in a complete suit of citizen's apparel, including an old fashioned three-cornered hat, which had been presented for that purpose."

In the personal character of Col. Willett, as has been justly remarked, "there were traits of chivalry and daring, so fearless and ardent, that in another age, he would have commanded the deepest and greatest admiration." Virtue, philanthropy and patriotism guided every step, and adorned every act of his eventful and public life; while in his private life he was distinguished for integrity, frankness and decision of character. Perhaps, however, the highest compliment that can be paid Col. Willett is, that in Judge Jones's *History of New York*, in which that gentleman assails with violence nearly all the actors in the events he describes, the worst he can say of him, after admitting that he was possessed of courage, is the remark quoted above regarding his being a principal leader of revolutionary mobs!

A son of Col. Willett is yet (1882) living near me on Jersey City Heights, N. J. He is still remarkably hale and hearty and in the full enjoyment of his physical and mental powers. He, it was, who, as a labor of filial piety, edited and published his father's *Narrative*. In a recent conversation with him he said that the engraving which forms the frontispiece of that work is a most miserable likeness of his father, in proof of which he showed me an exquisite sketch (in crayon) of the colonel, which certainly differs greatly from the engraving in the Narrative.

Mr. Willett also informed me that until lately (when they were stolen from him) he had in his possession some six original autograph letters from Washington to his father, two of which were couched in terms of warm commendation to Col. Willett for his successful sortie from Fort Stanwix.

Mr. Willett has long been favorably known as the author of works of a religious cast, he having written, among other books, The Life of Summerfield, The Life of the Messiah, The Restitution of all Things, etc. To see and converse, in the year of our Lord, 1882, with the son of an Indian fighter of the old French war, and a distinguished soldier of the Revolution, not only is a very great privilege, but brings the early colonial days vividly before the mind, making them indeed seem as of yesterday. (1)

(1) In this connection one cannot but recall another similar instance of a man who died but recently (1880), His name was Ransom Cook, of Saratoga Springs, whose father-in-law was Robert Ayers, the person who conveyed to Jane McCrea the message of her lover David Jones. Mr. Cook, who had become greatly distinguished by his many mechanical and scientific inventions, was, in many respects, a remarkable man, fully alive not only to the present, but to the past;

and when in the year of our Lord, 1880, we talked with him whose wife was the daughter of one who knew Jane McCrea intimately, past events no longer seemed dim and shadowy but actual realities!

The Frontiersmen of New York
by Jeptha R. Simms
Albany, NY 1883

Volume II, Page 491.

A Liaison of Col. Marinus Willett at Fort Plain.--Henry Seeber, a son of the pioneer tradesman, William Seeber, by his second marriage, is believed to have married Elizabeth, a daughter of John Lough, by whom he had two children, Jacob and Polly, who both grew up to be respected citizens; the latter, a fine looking girl, becoming the wife of Abram Lipe. Henry Seeber, who seems to have been an exception to the name of Seeber in this respect, became dissipated early in life, and like most of that class of men forfeited the respect of all good citizens; and although he had an education fitting him for a school teacher, he was troubled with a fever sore, was dissolute and improvident in his habits, all of which united led to an estrangement of the respect and affection of his wife, who was a proud and handsome woman.

At this stage in the affairs of this family, Col. Willett took command of Fort Plain, with an oversight of its adjacent military posts. The hero of Fort Stanwix was not long in discovering the charms of this woman of widowed affection, whose children were then small, and he not only made her acquaintance, but ere long was on most intimate terms with her, despite the busy tongue of scandal; and, in process of time, she presented her admiring hero with a young son, who took on the name of Marinus Willett Seeber. Whether or not this Henry Seeber house was "divided against itself", before the coming of the commandant of this frontier post I cannot say, but they were estranged ever after this event; and her son Jacob was taken by his uncle Conrad and reared to an honorable manhood. He also cared tenderly for Henry, an only son of his brother Audolph, who, then a widower was slain in the Oriskany battle.

This military waif was tenderly looked after by Col. Willett, who showed his manhood by placing him at school and defraying the expenses, somewhere, of his care and education until he arrived at manhood. When grown to man's estate he returned to Minden, and is remembered by my informant, then a boy, as a remarkably fine looking young man, and possessed of more than an ordinary intelligence. After his return to the Mohawk valley, he for a time taught a dancing school in Freysbush, and was known as Willett Seeber; but as his half brother and sister and other relatives did not recognize his kinship as he thought they should, he left the neighborhood and was ever after unknown to my informant.

(The venerable William H. Seeber, of Fort Plain, who was born in the present town of Minden, May 29, 1791. Mr. Seeber is a very intelligent gentleman and possessed of a remarkably good memory of the passing events of his early life. He is a great-grandson of William Seeber, Sen., elsewhere mentioned as the pioneer of that name, who came hither from Germany prior to the French war. His grandfathers, William Seeber, third son of William Seeber, Sen., by his first wife, married Elizabeth Sharron. Henry Seeber, his father, married Eve, a daughter of Thomas Casler. Informant has had two wives, Elizabeth and Nancy, daughters of Catharine Dygert (daughter of Warner Dygert, who was killed by the Indians at Fall Hill) and Henry Failing: both of whom he has outlived. Having been possessed of an inquisitive mind, he is not only a very companionable man, but looking back upon life, he is a good logical reasoner. He has ever been an exemplary man of remarkably good habits, ever honest and upright in his dealing, which accounts for his ripe old age. He is also a pensioner for services rendered his country in the war of 1812. NOTE--Mr. Seeber died in the spring of 1881, in the 90th year of his age.) This story was corroborated by others.

Life of Joseph Brant-Thayendanegea
Including the Indian Wars of the American Revolution
by William L. Stone. Volume II
Buffalo: Phinney & Co., 1851.

Chapter V

THE sun of the new year was veiled by a cloud of deeper gloom than had previously darkened the prospects of the American arms at any period of the contest. The whole army, in all its divisions, at the North and in the South, was suffering severely both for clothing and provisions. Indeed, the accumulated sufferings and privations of "the army constitute a large and interesting portion of the history of the war of American independence. At the date now under review, Winter, without much lessening the toils of the soldiers, was adding to their sufferings. They were perpetually on the point of starving, were often entirely without food, were exposed without "proper clothing to the rigors of the season; and had, moreover, "now served almost twelve months without pay." * Such was the general fact. The Pennsylvania troops had still farther grievances of which to complain. They had been enlisted in ambiguous terms-to "serve three years, or during the war." At the expiration of the stipulated period, "three years," the soldier claimed his discharge, while the officers insisted upon holding him to the other condition of the contract. The consequence was great dissatisfaction, increased, of course, by the much higher bounties subsequently paid for enlistments. The Pennsylvania line, consisting of six regiments, was cantoned at Morristown, under the immediate command of Brigadier General Wayne.

* Marshall's Life of Washington.

So long had they been brooding over their wrongs, so intense had become their sufferings, and so discouraging were the prospects of remedy or redress, that the discontents which, down to the last day of the preceding year, had only been nurtured, broke out into open mutiny on the evening of the next. The spirit of insubordination was from the first so decided, and the evidences of revolt were so general, as at once to jeopard the cause. An effort was made to quell the mutiny, in the course of which several of the turbulent soldiers were wounded, as also were some of the officers, who were endeavoring to repress the disorder. One of the officers, Captain Billings, was killed. But the cause of the revolt was too deeply seated, and the disaffection too extensive, to be easily overcome. Even Wayne himself, the favorite of the Pennsylvanians, was without power. Drawing a pistol and threatening one of the most turbulent of the revolters, a bayonet was presented at his own bosom.* In a word, the authority of the commissioned officers was at an end. The non-commissioned officers were generally engaged in the mutiny, and one of their number being appointed Commander-in-chief, they moved off in the direction of Philadelphia, with their arms and six pieces of artillery-deaf to the arguments, the entreaties, and the utmost efforts of their officers to change their purposes, + As a last resort, Wayne and his officers attempted to divide them, but without effect. Those who at first appeared reluctant, were soon persuaded to unite with their comrades, to march upon Philadelphia and demand a redress of their wrongs at the doors of Congress.

* Marshall

+ Letter of Washington to President Weare of New Hampshire. This was a letter urging upon the government of New Hampshire to make some exertion to relieve the distresses of the army. A circular was sent to all the New England States to the same effect, and confided to General Knox, as a special agent to enforce the appeal. To President Weare, the Commander-in-chief said, plainly ;-"I give it decidedly as my opinion, that it is in vain to think an army can be kept together much longer under such a variety of sufferings as ours has experienced; and that unless some immediate and spirited measures are adopted to furnish at least three months' pay to the troops in money, which will be of some value to them, and at the same time provide ways and means to clothe and feed them better than they have been, the worst that can befall us may be expected." The Legislatures of Massachusetts and New Hampshire nobly responded to the call, and immediately voted a gratuity of twenty-four dollars in hard money to each of the non-commissioned officers and soldiers belonging to those States, who were engaged to serve during the war.-Sparks.

The number of the revolters was about thirteen hundred-a loss that would have been severe of itself. But the most unpleasant apprehensions arose from the danger, not only that the spirit of insubordination might spread to other corps of the army, but that the mutineers might fall away in a body to the enemy, who would, of course, lose not a moment in availing himself of such a diversion in his favor. Coercive measures having failed to bring the revolters back to the path of duty, Wayne, with his principal officers, determined to follow close upon their rear, and after the first transports of their passion should subside, try what virtue might be found in the arts of persuasion. The General overtook them at night in the neighborhood of Middlebrook, but being advised in their present temper not to venture among them, he invited a deputation of one sergeant from each regiment to meet him in consultation. The deliberations were amicable, and the General suggested a mode of obtaining redress of their grievances, which satisfied the delegates, who, on retiring, promised to exert their influence in bringing the men back to duty. But the attempt was ineffectual; and on the day following the mutineers marched to Princeton-the few who were well disposed and willing to separate from the mutineers, continuing with the majority at the request of their officers; in the hope that their exertions might " moderate the violence of' their leaders, and check the contagion of their example."

The crisis was most critical. The Commander-in-chief, on receiving the first advices of the revolt, was disposed to repair at once to the camp of the mutineers; but on advisement and reflection, this course was relinquished. The complaints of the Pennsylvania line, in regard to destitution of provisions and clothing, were common to the whole army, and it was doubtful how far the contagion of disaffection might already have spread. Nor could the Commander-in-chief, whose head-quarters were at New Windsor, venture upon a visit to the mutineers, without taking with him a sufficient force to compel obedience to his commands should the exertion of force become necessary. But a sufficient body of troops for such an object could not be spared without leaving the fortresses in the Highlands too weak to resist an attack from Sir Henry Clinton, who would be sure to strike upon those important works at the first favorable moment. The river being free from ice, Sir Henry would possess every facility for such a movement the instant the back of Washington should be turned upon the North. Under all the circumstances of the case, therefore, the Commander-in-chief remained at his post, neglecting, however, no measure of justice within his power to heal the discontents, or of precaution to prevent their farther extension.

Meantime the mutineers remained several days at Princeton, refusing to proceed to the Delaware and cross into Pennsylvania, while Sir Henry Clinton made every disposition to avail himself of the revolt, and lost not a moment in despatching emissaries to their camp, with tempting offers to induce them to join the armies of the King. But, mutineers as they were, they nevertheless spurned the proposition; and retaining the emissaries in custody, handed the communications, of which they were the bearers, over to General Wayne. Though in rebellion against their officers, the soldiers were nevertheless indignant at the idea of turning their arms, as Arnold had done, against their own country; and those about them who were well disposed, availed themselves of the occasion, with much address, to impress upon their minds the magnitude of the insult conveyed in propositions made to them in the character of traitors.*

News of the revolt had no sooner reached Philadelphia, than a committee was appointed by Congress, consisting of General Sullivan,+ and two other gentlemen, in conjunction with President Reed on behalf of the Council of Pennsylvania, to meet the revolters, and attempt to bring them back to reason. The demands of the mutineers were exorbitant, but were in the end acceded to with some unimportant modifications. They then moved forward to Trenton, and in the end, although better things were anticipated from the stipulations agreed upon, the Pennsylvania line was almost entirely disbanded. A voluntary performance, by Congress, of much less than was yielded

*Five days after their arrival among the mutineers, viz. on the 11th of January, Sir Henry's emissaries were tried by a court-martial, and executed. + Very soon after he left the army, at the close of the Seneca campaign, General Sullivan was elected to Congress, of which body he was an efficient and patriotic member. Afterward, in the years 1786, 1787, and 1783, he was President of New Hampshire, in which situation, by his vigorous exertions, he quelled the spirit of insurrection which exhibited itself at the time of the troubles with Shays in Massachusetts. It 1782 he was appointed a District Judge. He died in 1795, aged 54.

by the committee, would have averted the evil, and saved the division.*

The success of the Pennsylvania mutineers induced the New Jersey line, then stationed at Pompton, to follow the bad example; and on the night of the 20th of January a large portion of the brigade rose in arms. Their claims were precisely the same as those which had been yielded to the Pennsylvanians. By this time, however, the Commander-in-chief had satisfied himself that he could rely upon the eastern troops; and, chagrined as he had been by the result of the Pennsylvania revolt, he determined, not only that nothing more should be yielded to the spirit of insubordination, but that such an example should be made as would operate as a check to the like proceedings in future. A strong detachment of troops was accordingly led against the insurgents by General Howe, with instructions to make no terms whatsoever while they continued in a state of resistance. General Howe was farther instructed to seize a few of the ringleaders, and execute them on the spot. The orders were promptly complied with, and the insurrection was crushed at a blow. The mutinous brigade returned to its duty; and such vigorous measures were taken by the States to supply the wants of the army, as effectually checked the progress of discontent.+ But it was only by the strong process of impressment that those supplies could be wrung from the people, whose discontents, though less immediately alarming, were, nevertheless, as great as had been those of the army.

The first active demonstration of Sir Henry Clinton, on the opening of the new year, was the expedition against Virginia, under the conduct of General Arnold. The arch-traitor had, in fact, sailed from New-York toward the close of December, but he did not enter the Capes of Virginia until the beginning of January-landing at Westover on the 5th. He marched to

---

*Although the Pennsylvania line was thus dissolved, the evil was surmountedmuch sooner than had been anticipated. Before the close of January, Wayne wrote to Washington that the disbanded soldiers were " as impatient of liberty as they had been of service, and that they were as importunate to be re-enlisted as they had been to be discharged." A reclaimed and formidable line was the result in the Spring.
+ Sir Henry Clinton endeavored to avail himself of this New Jersey insurrection, in like manner as he had attempted to tamper with the Pennsylvanians. But his emissary, who was in the American interest, delivered his papers to the first American officer with whom he met.

Richmond, and after some trifling skirmishes on the way, destroyed the stores at that place, and also at Westham; whereupon he retired to Norfolk. This was a mere predatory expedition, attended by no important result. Farther south, events were continually occurring of greater moment. General Greene having been assigned to the command of that department, after the signal discomfiture of Gates, affairs soon wore a brighter aspect.

The loss of the battle of Camden, a few months before, was balanced, and, in its moral effect, more than balanced, by the decisive victory over Tarleton, achieved by General Morgan at the Cowpens on the 17th of January. And although Greene was defeated at Guilford on the 15th of March, yet the victory was too dearly won by Earl Cornwallis to render it a just occasion of triumph. So likewise in the repulse of Greene by Lord Rawdon at Camden, owing to the misconduct of the militia, the British commander was nevertheless so roughly handled that, although he received a reinforcement in the course of the following night, he deemed it expedient to destroy the town, and retire farther down the Santee. But these apparent disadvantages were amply compensated by the masterly manoeuvres of Greene, and the brilliant succession of victories over the smaller works and detachments of the enemy. In these latter affairs, Forts Watkinson, Orangeburgh, Motte, Silver Bluff, Granby, and Cornwallis were successively taken, and the enemy was compelled to evacuate other forts. Lord Rawdon was likewise obliged to fall back upon Charleston, while Cornwallis was pursuing a doubtful march into Virginia. The great disadvantage labored under by General Greene, was the necessity of depending, in a great measure upon the militia-not having regular troops sufficient to cope with the veterans from Europe. But, though not always victorious in battle, he was invariably so in the results. And his masterly movements proved him far in advance of any of his antagonists, in all the requisites of an able commander.

But while events thus propitious to the American arms were occurring at the South, the aspect of affairs, as has already been seen, was sadly discouraging at the North. In addition to the destitution of the main army, causing the insurrections in the Pennsylvania and New-Jersey lines, so wretchedly supplied were the small garrisons from Albany northward and westward, both in respect to food and clothing, that it was only with the utmost difficulty that the officers could keep the soldiers upon duty. Ravaged as the whole Mohawk country had been the preceding' Summer and Autumn, no supplies could be drawn from the diminished and impoverished inhabitants remaining in those settlements; while it was equally difficult to procure supplies, either at Albany or below, or eastwardly beyond that city. It is painful to read the private correspondence of General Schuyler, and Governor and General Clinton upon this subject. Orders for impressing provisions were freely issued, particularly against the disaffected portion of the people, who had greatly increased in numbers in that section of the country; but some of the supplies thus taken were returned, from the knowledge of General Schuyler that they had nothing more for their own support. Meantime, emboldened by his successes the preceding year, the enemy hung around the skirts of the settlements, approaching almost beneath the very guns of the forts, cutting off all communication with them, unless by means of strong escorts, so that it was difficult and often impossible even to throw such scanty supplies into the garrisons as could be obtained.

The Oneidas having been driven from their country the preceding year, even the slight barrier against irruptions from the more western tribes, who were all hostile, into the Mohawk country, afforded by that slender people, was gone. On the 15th of January, the scouts of Thayendanegea appeared openly ill the German Flatts, and attacked some of the inhabitants. During the months of February and March, Brant was hovering about the Mohawk, ready to spring upon every load of supplies destined for Forts Plain, Dayton, and Schuyler, not too strongly guarded, and cutting off every straggling soldier or in habitant so unfortunate as to fall within his grasp.

On the 6th of March, Major Nicholas Fish wrote to General Clinton, from Schenectady, informing him that a party of fifteen of Colonel Van Cortlandt's regiment, at Fort Schuyler, had fallen into the hands of Brant's Indians; and on the 2d of April, in moving to the neighborhood of that fort, to cut off another escort of supplies, the same lynx-eyed chieftain made prisoners of another detachment from that garrison of sixteen men. The difficulty of transporting the provisions, however, the unbeaten snow lying to a great depth, had so greatly retarded the progress of the scouts, that the intrepid warrior was disappointed in this tempted to strike too soon.

But the hunted Oneidas, notwithstanding the neutrality of the greater part of them, were not altogether safe in their new position near Schenectady. It seems to have chafed both Brant and his employers; that a single tribe of Indians had been detached from their influence or service; and their destruction was again seriously meditated, with the sanction of Sir Frederick Haldimand, as will more fully appear by the annexed letter from Colonel Daniel Clans, the brother-in-law of Sir John Johnson, to Captain Brant.

COLONEL CLAUS TO CAPTAIN BRANT.
"Montreal, 3d March, 1781.
"DEAR JOSEPH,

"Captain John Odeserundiye, about a month ago, showed me a letter he received from you, with a proposal to him about the Oneidas, telling me he had answered you that he would join you with his party about the 20th of this month, desiring me at the same time to keep it a secret from the Mohawk Indians and others, for fear of being made public; he then asked me where the Oneidas now lived, which then I could not tell him; but since that I was informed that the rebels had posted themselves at a place called Palmerstown, about twelve or fifteen miles west of Saraghtoga, of which I acquainted His Excellency General Haldimand, together with your intentions and plan; whereupon I received His Excellency's answer enjoining the utmost secrecy to me, and which I hereby give you in the words of his letter, by Captain Mathews his secretary, and is the occasion of this express.

"His Excellency, General Haldimand, commands me to acquaint you that Captain Brant's intention meets highly with his approbation, and wishes to assist it; which might be done from this place in the following manner, but the General de sires you will keep it inviolably secret. He has for some time intended sending a party of about sixty chosen loyalists, under the command of Major Jessup, toward Fort Edward: this party might join Joseph against Palmerstown could he ascertain the time and place, which might be nearly done by calculating the time his express would take to come from Carleton Island-his march from thence, and Major Jessup's from Point au Fez, alias Nikadiyooni. If Joseph wishes to have this assistance, he must confer with Major Ross, who will send off an active express; otherwise, if Joseph should prefer aid from that quarter, Major Ross and Captain Robertson are directed to afford it; and, indeed, the delays and uncertainty of the parties joining punctually, incline the General to think it more eligible."

"Should you upon this adopt the General's offer and opinion, and proceed from Carleton Island to Palmerstown, which place I am sure several of Major Ross's men and others at the island are well acquainted with, I wish you the aid of Providence with all the success imaginable; in which case it will be one of the most essential services you have rendered your king this war, and cannot but by him be noticed and rewarded ; your return by Canada will be the shortest and most eligible, and we shall be very happy to see you here. As I received the General's letter this afternoon only, I could not speak with Odeserundiye, but have wrote to him by express to let you know the precise lime he intends meeting you. Mrs. Claus and all friends are well here, and salute you heartily; also your sister and daughters; the others here are well, and desire their love and duty. I hope she received the things safe which I sent lately by Anna Adieu. God bless and prosper you.

" Yours most sincerely,

" DAN'L. CLAUS.

" Captain Brant.

"P. S. The great advantage of setting out from Carleton Island, is the route, which is so unexpected a one, that there is hardly any doubt but you will surprise them, which is a great point gained. Whereas, were you to set out from Canada, there are so many friends, both whites and Indians, to the rebel cause, that you could not well get to the place undiscovered, which would not do so well. D" C."

Happily, from some cause now unknown, this project, so well devised, and apparently so near its maturity, Was never executed. The narrative is therefore resumed.

So great, and so universal, was the distress for provisions, already adverted to, that, on the 29th of March, General Clinton wrote to the Governor, "I am hourly under apprehensions that the remaining different posts occupied for the defence of the frontiers of this State, will be abandoned, and the country left open to the ravages of the enemy." Such continued suffering of course produced disaffection in this department also; and the greatest possible prudence was required, on the part of the officers, to prevent desertions of whole bodies. So critical was their situation, that in a letter to the Governor, of May 3d, General Clinton mentions the fact, that a small scout, commanded by a corporal, in the neighborhood of Fort George, having captured a party of the enemy, "with a packet, had been bribed to "release them for a guinea each and two silk handkerchiefs." Still worse than this was the fact that the General was afraid to proceed openly to punish the delinquency.

On the 5th General Clinton again wrote to the Governor-" From the present appearance, am convinced that the troops will abandon the frontier. It is absurd to suppose they can or will exist under the present circumstances. However, let what will be the consequences, I have nothing to reproach myself with. I have repeatedly called for assistance from every quarter, but could obtain none."

On the 8th of May, General Schuyler, writing from Saratoga, said-" I wrote you this morning, since which, finding the troops exceedingly uneasy, Colonel Van Vechten and I turned out each one of the best cattle we had; the meat proved better than was expected, but the soldiers still continue troublesome; they have hung part of it on a pole with a red flag above a white one, and some of them hold very alarming conversation. I dread the consequences, as they can so easily join the enemy. If a body of nine-months men were here, it would probably deter the others from going off to the northward, [the enemy meaning,] if they should have such an intendon."

Great blame was imputed to Congress, and likewise to the State governments, for allowing the commissariat to come to such a deplorable pass. The resources of the country were known to be abundant for the comfortable sustenance of a much larger army than was at that time in the field; but the efficient action of Congress was fettered by its want of power. The States, jealous of their own sovereignty, had withholden from the central government powers which were essential to the vigorous prosecution of the war, while it was but seldom that they could be brought into a simultaneous and harmonious exertion of those powers themselves. Hence the frequent and keen distresses of the army, and the complicated embarrassments under which the officers were compelled to struggle during the whole war. Still, the blame did not rest wholly with the States. There were jealousies, and heart-burnings, and intrigues, in the Congresses of that day, as in later times; and their conduct was often the subject of bitter complaint in the letters of the Commander-in-chief. The following letter from General Schuyler bears hard upon the officers of the federal government, while at the same time it depicts the extreme destitution of the country at the north, at the period under consideration:-

GENERAL SCHUYLER TO GENERAL CLINTON.
" Saratoga, May 13th, 1781.
" DEAR SIR,

"Your favor of the 8th instant, Captain Vernon delivered me last evening. The distress occasioned by the want of provisions in every quarter is truly alarming, but was the natural consequence of such a system as was adopted for supplying the army. It is probable, if we should be able to continue the war ten years longer, that our rulers will learn to conduct it with propriety and economy; at present they are certainly ignoramuses. Not a barrel of meat or fish is to be had in this quarter if an equal weight of silver was to be offered for it, and as there is not above a quarter of the flour or wheat sufficient for the use of the inhabitants, it would be needless to appoint persons here to impress those articles. I therefore return the blank warrants.

"It is probable that some flour may be obtained in the neighborhood of Schaghticoke, and 1 am certain that a very considerable quantity of both wheat and flour is lodged in Albany. Major Lush could employ his assistant at the former place, and he might impress all at the latter without much trouble. A small collection of meat has been made at Stillwater for the troops here, but that is already expended. If there is any beef at Richmond, or Barrington, I think it would be well to send a party of nine-months men under an active spirited officer, to impress a number of wagons at Kinderhook and Claverack, and to attend them to the former places, and back again to the respective landings of the latter on Hudson's river. If an opportunity comes, pray send me some paper, as this is my last sheet. Captain Arson is not yet returned from Jessup's.

" I am, dear Sir,
" Yours sincerely, &c. &c.
" PH. SCHUYLER.
" Gen. Clinton."

It was, indeed, a trying situation for brave and patriotic officers to find themselves in command of troops, driven, by destitution, to the very point of going over to the enemy almost in a body. But another disheartening occurrence was at hand. The works of Fort Schuyler, having become much out of repair, sustained great injury by the swelling of the waters in the early part of May. A council of officers was convened by Lt. Colonel Cochran, then in command, on the 12th of that month, to inquire and report what should be done in the premises. The council represented that more than two-thirds of the works had been broken down by the flood, and that the residue would be in the same condition in a very few days ; that the only remaining strength of the fort was to be found in the outside pickets on the glacis; and that the strength of the garrison was altogether inadequate to attempt to rebuild or repair the works, for which purpose five or six hundred men, with an engineer, artificers, &c. would be indispensably necessary.

But even if the works were not altogether indefensible on the 12th, they were rendered so on the following day, when all that had been spared by the deluge was destroyed by fire. Intelligence of this disaster was received by General Clinton at Albany, on the 16th, in a letter from Colonel Cochran- The following is an extract from General Clinton's reply to that officer, from which it appears a strong suspicion was entertained that the conflagration was the work of design-a suspicion that was never removed:-" I have just received your favors of the 13th and 14th instants, with the disagreeable intelligence contained in them. I cannot find words to express my surprise at the unexpected accident, or how a fire should break out at noonday, in a garrison where the troops could not possibly be absent, after a most violent and incessant rain of several days, and be permitted to do so much damage.

I am sorry to say that the several circumstances which accompanied this melancholy affair, afford plausible ground for suspicion that it was not the effect of mere accident. I hope, when it comes to be examined in a closer point of view, such lights may be thrown upon it as will remove the suspicion, for which there appears too much reason. I have written to his Excellency on the subject, and requested his farther orders, which I expect in a few days; in the meantime I would request that you keep possession of the works, and endeavor to shelter the troops in the best manner possible."

In his letter to the Governor, enclosing the dispatches of Colonel Cochran, General Clinton suggested the expediency, under the circumstances of the case, of abandoning the post altogether, and falling back upon Fort Herkimer. On the following day he again wrote to his brother, renewing and re-enforcing this suggestion:-

GENERAL CLINTON TO THE GOVERNOR.
"Albany, May 17th, 1781.
"DEAR SIR,

"Since my last to you of yesterday, another letter, by express, has been received from Fort Schuyler. Copies of the contents I enclose for your information, under cover, which I wish you to seal and forward to the Commander-in-chief. I informed you yesterday of the general prevailing opinion among the better part of the people in this quarter respecting Fort Schuyler. The recent loss of the barracks, and the ruinous situation of the works, have confirmed them in the propriety and even necessity of removing it to the German Flatts near Fort Herkimer, where they are disposed to afford every assistance in their power to build a formidable work, confident that it will be able to afford more protection, not only in that particular quarter, but also to the whole western frontier in general. I must confess that I have long since been of this opinion. I have not mentioned this circumstance to the General, [Washington,] as I conceive it will come better from yourself, as you are acquainted with every particular circumstance respecting it, and the numberless difficulties which we shall labor under in putting it in any considerable state of defence. As I have directed the troops to remain in possession of the works until 1 shall receive instructions from head-quarters, I wish that you might have it in your power to have a conference with the General on the subject, and transmit to me the result of it without delay. I am, Sir, &c."

"JAS. CLINTON.

"Governor Clinton."

This suggestion was adopted, and the post so long considered the key to the Mohawk Valley was abandoned.*

In addition to still disheartening state of affairs at the westward of Albany, intelligence was received that another storm was about breaking upon the northern frontier. In a letter from General Schuyler to General Clinton, from Saratoga, May 18th, after speaking of the "chagrin" he felt at the destruction of the fort, Schuyler proceeds:-

"Last evening Major McCracken of White Creek came here, and delivered me a copy of a paper which had been found there, in the same hand-writing as one that was put in the same place last year, announcing the approach of Major Carleton with the troops under his command. This contains in substance-' That the writer had received a letter from a friend in Canada, to give him notice of the danger which threatened these parts; that 1500 men were gone to Ticonderoga, from whence they were to proceed to Fort Edward and White Creek; that they are to be down in this month, and from what he could learn, they were to desolate thc country.' The Major thinks he knows the channel through which this intelligence is conveyed, and that it may be depended upon ;- as it in some degree corroborates that given by Harris, and the person I had sent to Crown Point, it ought not to be slighted. Please to communicate it to the Governor and General Washington.

"Fourteen of the nine months men have already deserted, two of whom are apprehended. There are now at this post only thirty-nine of them. As the Continental troops here are without shoes, it is impossible to keep out the necessary scouts. Can-

* After the war the fort was rebuilt, and the ancient name of Fort Stanwix restored. The works were repaired and essentially strengthened, as being an important post, during the administration of the elder Adams.

not a parcel of shoes be obtained at Albany, and sent up to them?

It will be of importance to give the earliest intelligence if the party discovered by Colonel Lewis should appear on the Mohawk river, that we may with the troops here, and what militia we may be able to collect, try to intercept them."

In a postscript to a letter of the 21st, General Schuyler observed :-"Since the above I have been informed from very good authority, that the enemy's morning and evening guns at Ticonderoga have been distinctly heard near Fort Anne for three or four days past." And on the 24th the General wrote more confidently still of the enemy's approach. Captain Gray is returned. He has not been near enough to determine the enemy's force, but sufficiently so to discover, by the fires, that they are numerous. Is it not strange, and subject of suspicion, that the Vermonters should not afford us any intelligence of the enemy's approach, as they must certainly know of his arrival at Crown Point and Ticonderoga?"*

This was alarming intelligence, more especially when taken in connexion with the reports simultaneously coming in from the west, of an expedition meditated against Pittsburgh, to be led by Sir John Johnson and Colonel Connelly; while other reports were rife, at the same time, of more extensive combinations among the hostile Indians than had previously marked the war.

But even this was not all-nor by any means the worst of the case. Treachery was at work, and from the temper of great numbers of the people, the carriage of the disaffected, and the intelligence received by means of spies and intercepted despatches, there was just cause to apprehend that, should the enemy again invade the country, either from the north or the west, his standard would be joined by much larger numbers of the people than would have rallied beneath it at any former period. The poison was actively at work even in Albany. On the

24th of May, General Schuyler announced to General Clinton the return of a confidential agent from the

* This ambiguous conduct of Vermont was the consequence of the quarrel-between the settlers of the grants from New Hampshire, which were within the chartered limits, and the government of New-York. Colonel Allen, not long before, had been in Albany upon the business of the settlers, and had gone away dissatisfied-having uttered a threat on his departure. He was at this lime, as General Schuyler was informed, at the Isle Au Noix-sick-as was pretended.

north, " where he met with five of the enemy, whose confidence he so far obtained as to be entrusted with letters written on the spot to persons at Albany, whose names I forbear to mention," (says Schuyler,) " for fear of accidents. They contained nothing material, except the arrival of the enemy in force at Crown Point and Ticonderoga, with this expression in one,-' We shall make rare work with the rebels.' " But other, and more " material" despatches were soon afterward intercepted, from the tenor of which the conclusion was irresistible, not only that a powerful invasion was about taking place from the north, but that very extensive arrangements had been made in Albany, and the towns adjacent, for the reception of the invaders, whose standard thc disaffected were to join, and whose wants they were to supply. Among the papers thus intercepted, was the following letter, supposed to have been addressed to General Haldimand:-
"Albany, 9th May, 1781.

"Your Excellency may learn from this that when I received your instructions, &c., I was obliged at that time to put myself into a place of security, as there were heavy charges laid against me. I thank God I have baffled that storm. Your commands are observed to the letter, part of them faithfully executed, the particulars of which I hope in a short time to have the honor to acquaint yon verbally. Now is the season to strike a blow on this place, when multitudes will join, provided a considerable force comes down. The sooner the attempt is made the better. Let it be rapid and intrepid, carefully avoiding to sour the inhabitants' tempers by savage cruelties on their defenceless families. If a few handbills, intimating pardon, protection, &c. &c. were sent down, and distributed about this part of the country, they would effect wonders; and should your Excellency think proper to send an army against this den of persecutors, notice ought to be given ten days before, by some careful and intelligent person, to a certain Mr. McPherson in Ball'sTowny who will immediately convey the intention to the well-affected of New Scotland, Norman's Kill, Hillbarack's, Neskayuna, &c., all in the vicinity of Albany. The plan is already fixed, and should a formidable force appear, I make no doubt provisions and other succors will immediately take place. A few lines of comfort, in print, from your Excellency to those people; would make them the more eager in prosecuting their designs; and if the Vermonters lie still, as I have some hopes they will, there is no fear of success. No troops are yet raised. There is a flag from this place shortly to be sent; perhaps I may go with it; I expected before this time I would be removed from my present situation, &c

"25th May. N.B. This I expected should reach you before now, but had no opportunity. Excuse haste." *

Accompanying this letter were several pages of memoranda, in the same hand-writing, giving particular information upon every point which the enemy could desire. The deplorable situation of Albany, and the whole Mohawk country, was described; the temper of the people in the towns around Albany and elsewhere set forth; the strength of the main army in the Highlands given with all necessary accuracy; and the mission of Ethan Allen to Albany, and the probable defection of Vermont, announced. Indeed, the character of these communications showed but too plainly that treason was deeply and extensively at work, and that the enemy was, beyond doubt, correctly advised of the true situation of the country.+

Under all these circumstances of internal and external danger-with but slender garrisons at the points of greatest exposure, and those so miserably provided that the soldiers were deserting by dozens, showing dispositions not equivocal of going over to the enemy-without provisions or the means of procuring them, and scarcely knowing whom to trust among their own people, lest the disaffection should prove to be even more extensive

* This document has been discovered by the author among the papers of General Clinton. It is endorsed as follows:-"A copy of a letter in Doctor Smyth's handwriting, supposed to General Haldimand. Intercepted 27th of May, 178I." The author has not been able to ascertain who Doctor Smith was, farther than that he has been informed it Albany, that he was a brother to Smith the historian of New-York, afterward Chief Justice of New Brunswick. Some time afterward Governor Clinton transmitted a special message to the legislature, then sitting at Poughkeepsie, containing important information respecting the designs of the Vermonters, by which it appears that Dr. Smith was actively engaged in fomenting disaffection in that quarter, and had held interviews with Ethan Allen upon the subject in Albany, &c. Smith is spoken of in that message as having been appointed a Commissioner by the British officers to treat with the Vermonters.

than recent disclosures had taught the officers to suppose,- the Spring of 1781 may well be counted as the darkest period of o the revolution. Had it not been for the gleams of light shooting up from the south, all indeed would have been sullen blackness, if not despair. But the truth of the homely adage, that the darkest hour is always just before day, received a glorious illustration before the close of the year. "Accustomed to contemplate all public events which might grow out of the situation of the United States, and to prepare for them while at a distance, the American chief was not depressed by this state of affairs. With a mind happily tempered by nature and improved by experience, those fortunate events which had occasionally brightened the prospects of his country, never relaxed his exertions or lessened his precautions; nor could the most disastrous state of things drive him to despair."

* Fortunately, in the Clintons and their associate officers at the north, the American Commander had subordinates possessing in no small degree the same

great characteristics. Every possible precaution against lurking treason within, was taken, and every practicable means of preparation and defence against invasion from abroad, was adopted.

Anticipating, from the presence of the enemy at Ticonderoga, that Tryon county might again be attacked from that direction by the way of the Sacondaga, Captain John Carlisle was despatched into the settlements of New Galway, Peasley, and Ballston; accompanied by Captain Oothout and a small party of Indians, to make prisoners of certain persons suspected of disaffection to the American cause, and to remove all the families from those towns to the south side of the Mohawk river. About sixty families were thus removed, and all the suspected persons arrested. The Captain, in his report of the expedition, gave a deplorable account of the poverty of the people. He could scarcely procure subsistence for his party during his mission. On arriving at Ballston, however, he drew more liberally upon the stores of the disaffected, and then arrested them. But their disposition, Captain Oothout was glad to inform the Commissioners, was such as to "prevent his setting fire to their houses agreeably to the letter of his orders."+ Happily these measures

*Marshall.

+Manuscripts of Gen. Clinton. Indeed, the materials for this whole section of the northern history of the Spring of 1781, have principally been drawn from the Clinton papers, so often referred to, of precaution, and the other preparations, were for that time unnecessary-the enemy, if he was in actual force at Crown Point or Ticonderoga, not then venturing another invasion from that quarter.

But the Mohawk Valley was continually harassed by the Indians and Tories-even to the very precincts of the stockades and other small fortifications. The spirit of the people had in a great measure been crushed, and the militia broken down, during the repeated invasions of the preceding year. The Rev. Daniel Gros,* writing to General Clinton from Canajoharie, upon the importance of having at least a small detachment of regular troops at Fort Rensselaer, observed-" It would serve to bring spirit, order, and regularity into our militia, where authority and subordination have vanished. If it should last a little longer, the shadow of it will dwindle away; and perhaps the best men in the state will be useless spectators of all the havoc the enemy is meditating against the country. The militia appears to me to be a body without a soul. Drafts from the neighboring counties, even of the levies under their own commanders, will not abate the fatal symptoms, but rather serve to produce a monster with as many heads as there are detachments." Having no other defenders than such as are here described, with the exception of a few scattered companies, or rather skeletons of companies, at the different posts extending along the Valley, the prospect of the opening Summer was indeed gloomy-more especially when men's thoughts reverted to the sufferings of the past. Nor were the inhabitants encouraged to expect any considerable reinforcements from head-quarters, since the Commander-in-chief, in concert with the Count de Rochambeau, was again evidently preparing for some enterprise of higher moment than the defence of those remote settlements against any force that could be brought down upon them from the north.

Still, there was one officer whose name, among the people of that district, was a tower of strength. That man was Colonel Marinus Willett; who, at the consolidation of the five New-York

* Afterward a Professor in Columbia College, and author of a work on Moral Philosophy.

regiments into two-an event happening at about the same time-was induced by the strong solicitation of Governor Clinton to take the command of all the militia levies and State troops that might be raised for the protection of the country.

It was only with great reluctance that Colonel Willett was persuaded to leave the main army, and enter upon this difficult and hazardous service. But the appeal of Governor Clinton was so strong and enforced with so much earnestness, that he could not resist it. The Governor urged the high confidence reposed in him by the people of Tryon county-and reminded him of the cruelties of the Indians and Tories-speaking of the latter with great emphasis, as "cruel monsters worse than savages;" *and Colonel Willett, feeling a hearty good-will to chastise such an enemy-the Tories especially-repaired to the north, and assumed the command. He arrived at Fort Rensselaer (Canajoharie), where he established his head-quarters, toward the close of June. The country he was to defend embraced all the settlements west of the county of Albany, including Catskill and the Hudson river. A fortnight after his arrival he ascertained that the following skeleton detachments composed the full complement of the forces under his command: one hundred and thirty levies, including officers, and Captain Moody's artillery, numbering twenty men, at the German Flatts; at Schoharie he stationed a guard of twenty men; at Catskill about the same number, and about thirty men at Ballston. Exclusive of these diminutive fragments of corps, stationed at great distances apart, the levies of the county amounted to no more than ninety-six men. In a letter to Governor Clinton, making known the paucity of his numbers, Colonel Willett added:-" I confess myself not a little disappointed in having such a trifling force for such extensive business as I have on my hands; and also that nothing is done to enable me to avail myself of the militia. The prospect of a suffering country hurts me. Upon my own account I am not uneasy. Every thing I can do, shall be done ; and more cannot be looked for. If it is, the reflection that I have done my duty, must fix my own tranquillity."+

Depressed, however, as were the people, and inefficient as, from the preceding descriptions, the militia must have become

---

* "Willett's Narrative.
+ Idem.

---

these circumstances were, no doubt, in a great degree attributable to the want of officers in whom the people could repose confidence. Colonel Willett had very soon an opportunity to make trial of their spirit, and he found them " a people who, having experienced no inconsiderable portion of British barbarism, "were become keen for revenge and properly determined."* The occasion was the following:-On the 30th of June, several columns of smoke were discovered by the garrison of Fort Rensselaer, ascending as from a village on fire, in the direction of Currietown, lying eleven miles down the river, near the estuary of the Schoharie-kill. Having previously sent forth a scout of thirty men, commanded by Captain Gross, to patrol the country south as far as a settlement called Durlagh,+- an express was despatched to overtake that officer, with information of the probable presence of the enemy below, and with instructions, if possible, to fall upon his trail. Meantime Captain M'Kean was ordered to Currietown, with sixteen levies only, but with instructions to collect as many of the militia in his way as possible. Such was the celerity of M'Kean's movements, that he arrived at Currietown so soon after it had been ravaged and deserted by the enemy, as to enable him to assist in quenching the fires of some of the yet unconsumed buildings. Colonel Willett was himself actively employed during the day in collecting the militia, while, through the vigilance of Captain Gross, not only the trail of the Indians was discovered, but the place of their encampment. Having reason to suppose they would occupy the same encampment that night, and being joined before evening by the detachments of Gross and M'Kean, the Colonel determined, with these forces, and such few militia-men as he had been able to collect, to march directly for the encampment, and, if possible, take them by surprise before morning-perhaps while asleep. This encampment was in a thick cedar swamp, five or six miles to the north-east of Cherry Valley, and of course to reach it by a march through the woods, during an exceedingly dark night, and without, any better road than a bridle-path, was no small undertaking. It had been ascertained that the Indians numbered between two and three hundred, commanded by a Tory named John Doxstader, in connexion with an Indian

*Letter of Colonel Willett to General Washington.
+ Sometimes spelt Turlock. Now the town of Sharon, Schoharie County.

chief named Quackyack. Colonel Willett's strength, levies and militia included, did not exceed one hundred and fifty rank and file.

The plan of falling upon the enemy while asleep did not exactly succeed, in consequence of the difficulties of the march-occasioned by the darkness, the thickness of the woods, and, worse than all, the losing of his way by the guide. It was therefore nearly six o'clock in the morning when they arrived in the vicinity of the encampment; and, instead of falling upon the enemy by surprise, they found him occupying a more favorable situation, and awaiting their reception.

Immediate dispositions were made to engage the enemy, with a view to which a stratagem was laid to draw him from the advantageous situation which he had chosen. For this purpose, before the Indians had become fully aware of Willett's near approach, Jacob Sammons, now a lieutenant in the New-York levies, was detached with ten resolute men, to steal as near to them as possible, give them one well-directed fire, and retreat.

The ruse succeeded. Sammons and his men turned their backs on the first yell of the Indians, and the latter sprang forward in pursuit.* They were soon met by Colonel Willett in person, advancing at the head of his main division, which consisted of one hundred men, while Captain M'Kean was left with fifty more as a reserve, to act as occasion might require, on the right.

The enemy did not wait an attack, however, but, with great appearance of determination, advanced with their wonted shouts and yells, and began the fire. The onset of the Indians was furious; but they were received with firmness, and in turn the Americans advanced upon them with loud huzzas, and such manifestations of spirit as soon caused them to give way. Simultaneously with their attack upon the main body in front, the

Indians had made an equally desperate rush upon the right wing, which might have been attended with disaster, but for the destructive fire poured in upon them by the reserve of M'Kean. The Indians, thus driven back, now betook themselves to their old game of firing from behind the trees; but Willett's men understood that mode of fighting as well as themselves. They did not, however, practice it long. Willett pressed forward waving his hat and cheering his men-calling

*MS. Narrative of Jacob Sammons.

out that he could catch in his hat all the balls that the enemy might send; and in the same breath exclaiming, "the day is ours, my boys!" These inspiriting demonstrations being followed up by a timely and efficient use of the bayonet, the whole body of the enemy was put to flight in half an hour after the commencement of the action.

They retreated upon their old path down the Susquehanna, and were pursued to a considerable distance. Their camp was, of course, taken, and the plunder they had gathered recaptured. The loss of the Indians was severe-nearly forty of their dead being left on the field. Colonel Willett's loss was five killed, and nine wounded and missing. Among the wounded was the brave Captain M'Kean, fatally. He received two balls early in the engagement, but kept at his post until it was over, and the rout of the enemy complete*.

There was one very painful circumstance attending this battle. In their excursion to Currietown, the day before, Doxstader and his Indians had made nine prisoners, among whom were Jacob and Frederick Diefendorff, Jacob Myers and a son, a black boy, and four others. The moment the battle commenced, the prisoners, who were bound to standing trees for security, were tomahawked and scalped by their captors, and left as dead. The bodies of these unfortunate men were buried by Colonel Willett's troops. Fortunately, however, the graves were superficial, and the covering slight-a circumstance which enabled Jacob Diefendorff, who, though stunned and apparently dead, was yet alive, to disentomb himself. A detachment of militia, under Colonel Veeder, having repaired to the field of action after Willett had returned to Fort Rensselaer, discovered the supposed deceased on the outside of his own grave; and he has lived to furnish the author of the present work with an account of his own burial and resurrection.+

Captain M'Kean died, greatly lamented, a few days after the detachment had returned to the fort, as will be seen by the annexed letter, addressed by Colonel Willett to the commanding officer at Albany:-

---

* Willett's Narrative-Campbell.
+ Statements of Jacob Diefendorff and Jacob Sammons, in the author's possession.

COLONEL WILLETT TO GENERAL CLINTON.

"SIR:-I have just sent some of the wounded levies to Schenectady, there being no surgeon here. Doctor Petrie, the surgeon of the levies, is at German Flatts, where he has several sick and wounded to attend; and the intercourse between here and there is too dangerous to allow travelling without a guard. I could wish, therefore, to have a surgeon from the hospital posted in this quarter.

"This -place does not afford a gill of rum to bathe a single wound The two barrels designed for this quarter a few days ago, met with a regular regiment passing down the country, who very irregularly took away from the person that had them in charge those two barrels of rum. I need not mention to you, Sir, that the severe duty and large portion of fatigue that falls to the lot of the troops in this quarter, make rum an article of importance here, and that I should be glad to see some in the County of Tryon.

"This morning Captain M'Kean died of the wound he received yesterday. In him we have lost an excellent officer. I feel his loss, and must regret it."*

Shortly after the irruption of Doxstader, there was another descent of Indians and Tories upon Palatine, which was an event of more singularity than importance. A son of Colonel Jacob Klock, with several of his Tory friends, went off to Canada. He returned in about four weeks with a band of Indians and Tories to fall upon the settlement; and encamped for one night in the vicinity of his own neighborhood. During the night, one of the number, Philip Helmer, having discovered that a part of their object was to plunder and murder the family of his relative, John Bellinger, determined to save that family. Taking a young Indian with him, therefore, under the pretext of reconnoitering the settlement, he proceeded so near to some of the houses, that the Indian, becoming suspicious, ran back to his comrades. Helmer's object was to surrender himself, and cause the Indian to be taken prisoner; and he accordingly delivered himself up to Judge Nellis. Expresses were immediately sent to Fort Plain and Stone Arabia for assistance; and the enemy, finding themselves betrayed, took to the woods. Lieutenant;

*Clinton papers.

and so rapid were they of foot, as to arrive at the enemy's encampment before his fires had gone out. William Feeter, with six other volunteers, was sent forward to keep his trail. In about two miles after entering the woods, most luckily they discovered a number of the Indians lying flat upon the ground. The latter no sooner discerned Feeter's approach, than they rose and fired; but one of their number having fallen grievously wounded by the return fire of Feeler's party, while they were stooping down to re-load, they sprang to their feet and fled-Tories and all-leaving their provisions, knapsacks, and some of their muskets. They ran down a steep hill, and were measurably shielded from Feeter's fire by the thickness of the shrubbery and trees. One of them gave himself up as a prisoner; three more were wounded, and died on their way to Canada. The poor Indian first wounded, was put to death by Helmer, who ran up and despatched him while he was begging for quarter!*

Colonel Willett took early occasion to make the Commander-in-chief acquainted with the deplorable situation to which this fine region of country had been reduced by the repeated visitations of the enemy. In his letter to General Washington upon the subject, he describes the beauty, the productiveness, and the natural advantages of the country with, a glowing pen. From this communication it appears, that at the commencement of the war, the number of enrolled militia in Tryon county amounted to not less than two thousand five hundred; but at the date of the letter, (July 6, 1781,) the number of inhabitants liable to pay taxes, or to be assessed to raise men for the public service, was estimated at no more than twelve hundred; while the number liable to bear arms did not exceed eight hundred. To account for so large a reduction of the population, it was estimated that one-third had been killed or made prisoners; one-third had gone over to the enemy; and one-third, for the time being, had abandoned the country. The situation of those that remained, the Colonel described as so distressing as to provoke sympathy from even the most unfeeling heart. Those who could afford

---

* Narrative of Colonel "William Feeter, in the author's possession, and also of Jacob Sammons. Colonel Feeter is yet living, (1837.)

---

the expense, or perform the labor, had erected block-houses on their own farms, for the protection of their families. Each neighborhood had been compelled to erect a fortification for itself, within which their families resided for safety-from ten to fifty families crowding together in a fort. Of these works there were twenty-four between Schenectady and Fort Schuyler. At the time of writing this letter-or rather memoir, for the communication was extended through several sheets-Colonel Willett stated that the whole number of men then under his command, exclusive of the militia, did not exceed two hundred and fifty. But he, nevertheless, kept up a good heart, and in the course of his anticipations of bringing about a better state of things, added- "Nor shall I exceed my hopes, if, in the course of less "than twelve months, I shall be able to convince the enemy that they are not without vulnerable quarters in these parts." The following quotation will illustrate alike the wisdom, the activity, and the skill of the dispositions made by Willett, for the purpose not only of bringing order out of confusion, but of displaying his strength before an invisible foe, lurking stealthily about in every place of concealment, on all sides and every hand.

After stating that he had fixed his head-quarters at Canajoharie, on account of its central position, he proceeds:- "My intention is to manage business so as to have an opportunity of acquainting myself, as well as possible, with every officer and soldier I may have in charge. In order the better to do this, I propose, as far as I can make it any way convenient, to guard the different posts by detachments, to be relieved as the nature of the case will admit.

"And as the relieved troops will always return to Fort Rensselaer, where my quarters will be, I shall have an opportunity of seeing them all in turn. Having troops constantly marching backward and forward through the country, and frequently changing their route, will answer several purposes, such as will easily be perceived by you, sir, without mentioning them. This is not the only way by which I expect to become particularly acquainted with the troops and their situation. I intend occasionally to visit every part of the country, as well to rectify such mistakes as are common among the kind of troops I have at present in charge, as to enable me to observe the condition of the militia, upon whose aid I shall be under the necessity of placing considerable reliance."

The effect of Colonel Willett's presence and example was very soon perceptible. The people reposed the most unlimited confidence in him; and so rapidly did he infuse something of his own fire and energy into the bosoms even of the dispirited and broken militia, that they presently appeared like a different race of men. An illustration of this fact occurred one night early in July. The Colonel was informed, at the hour of one o'clock in the morning, of -the presence of fifty or sixty Indians and Tories in the neighborhood, at only about six miles distance. Having barely troops enough in the fort to guard it, he sent immediately for a Captain of the militia, and in one hour's time that officer was in search of the enemy at the head of seventy men. It is not often that much good results from the employment of militia. Few officers can do any thing with them. Most commanders nothing. But Willett was an exception in those days, as General Jackson has been since. Willett, like Jackson, possessed the faculty, by looking into the eyes of his men, of transfusing his own native fire into their bosoms in spite of themselves.

Fortunately, however, less trouble was experienced from the enemy during the Summer, in the lower section of the Mohawk Valley, than had been anticipated. The summary and severe chastisement inflicted upon Doxstader and his party had a powerful effect upon that irritating branch of the enemy's service; and for more than three months afterward the inhabitants were only troubled occasionally, and then merely by small flying parties of the enemy, who accomplished nothing worthy of record. But in the upper section of the Valley, the German Flatts, it was otherwise, and several spirited affairs occurred in that neighborhood, attended by great bravery, though not by important consequences.

The name of Solomon Woodworth has twice or thrice occurred in the preceding pages; once, as having been taken a prisoner and making his escape, and again as alone defending a block-house north of Johnstown, and repulsing the enemy from his fortress. In the year 1781 he was commissioned a captain, for the purpose of raising a company of rangers to traverse the wooded country north of Fort Dayton and the German Flatts. He succeeded in enlisting a company of forty brave and kindred spirits; at the head of whom; well armed and provided, he marched from Fort Dayton, striking in the direction of the Royal Grant,* for purposes of observation. After a few hours' march, one of Woodworth's men, being a short distance in advance, discovered an Indian, evidently in ambuscade, upon whom he immediately fired. Instantly the forest resounded with the war-whoop, and Woodworth with his little band, was surrounded by doable his own number. A furious and bloody engagement followed, in which the Rangers and Indians fought hand to hand with great desperation; and, for the numbers engaged, there was cruel slaughter. A fiercer engagement, probably, did not occur during the war. Woodworth fell dead. The savages were the victors; and of the rangers, only fifteen escaped to tell the melancholy fate of their comrades. Several were taken captive, and subsequently exchanged.+

Another affair, as an individual exploit, was as remarkable for its coolness and bravery, as for the singular incident occurring: in the course of the battle, or rather siege, by which the leader of the enemy was made to supply ammunition to be used against his own troops. There was, and is to this day, a wealthy German settlement about four miles north of the village of Herkimer, called Shell's Bush. Among those of the settlers who had built block-houses of their own, was John Christian Shell. His Stockade was large and substantial, and well calculated for defence. The first story had no windows, but small loop-holes, through which the inmates could fire upon any persons venturing to assail them. The second story projected two or three feet over the first, so constructed that the garrison could either fire upon those who approached too near, or cast down missiles upon their heads. Shell had a family of six sons, the youngest two of whom were twins and but eight years old. In the afternoon of the 6th of August, Donald M'Donald, one of the Scotch refugees who fled from Johnstown, made an attack upon Shell's Bush at the head of a band of sixty-six Indians and Tories, among the latter of whom were two celebrated traitors, named Empie and Kassellman.++ Most of the inhabitants of Shell's Bush, however; had taken refuge in Fort Dayton-four miles distant: but John Christian Shell, being a sturdy believer in the doctrine

* A large tract of land, so called from the fact that it was a grant from the King, under his own sign manual, to Sir William Johnson.
+Manuscripts of the Rev. John I. Shew.
++MS. notes of Lauren Ford.

that every man's house is his castle, refused to quit his own domicile. He and his sons -were at work in the field when M'Donald and his party made their appearance; and the children were unfortunately separated so widely from their father, as to fall into the hands of the enemy. Shell and his other boys succeeded in reaching their castle, and barricading the ponderous door. And then commenced the battle. The besieged were well armed, and all behaved with admirable bravery; but none more bravely than Shell's wife, who loaded the pieces as her husband and sons discharged them.

The battle commenced at two o'clock, and continued until dark. Several attempts were made by M'Donald to set fire to the castle, but without success; and his forces were repeatedly driven back by the galling fire they received. M'Donald at length procured a crow-bar and attempted to force the door; but while thus engaged he received a shot in the leg from Shell's blunderbuss, which put him *hors du combat.*

None of his men being sufficiently near at the moment to rescue him, Shell, quick as lightning, opened the door, and drew him within the walls a prisoner. The misfortune of Shell and his garrison was, that their ammunition began to run low; but M'Donald was very amply provided, and to save his own life, he surrendered his cartridges to the garrison to fire upon his comrades. Several of the enemy having been killed and others wounded, they now drew off for a respite. Shell and his troops, moreover, needed a little breathing time; and feeling assured that, so long as he had the commanding officer of the besiegers in his possession, the enemy would hardly attempt to burn the citadel, he ceased firing. He then went up stairs, and sang the hymn which was a favorite of Luther during the perils and afflictions of the Great Reformer in his controversies with the Pope.* While thus engaged, the enemy likewise ceased firing. But they soon afterward rallied again to the fight, and made a desperate effort to carry the fortress by assault. Rushing up to the walls, five of them thrust the muzzles of their guns through the loop-holes, but had no sooner done so, than Mrs. Shell, seizing an axe, by quick and well-directed blows ruined every musket thus thrust through the walls, by bending the barrels! A few

* A literal translation of this hymn has been furnished the author by Professor Bokum of Harvard University, which will be found in No. III, of the Appendix.

more well-directed shots by Shell and his sons once more drove the assailants back. Shell thereupon ran up to the second story, just in the twilight, and calling out to his wife with a loud voice, informed her that Captain Small was approaching from Fort Dayton with succors. In yet louder notes he then exclaimed-" Captain Small, march your company round upon this side of the house. Captain Getman, you had better wheel your men off to the left, and come up upon that side."

There were, of course, no troops approaching; but the directions of Shell were given with such precision, and such apparent earnestness and sincerity, that the stratagem succeeded, and the enemy immediately fled to the woods, taking away the twin-lads as prisoners.* Setting the best provisions they had before their reluctant guest, Shell and his family lost no time in repairing to Fort Dayton, which they reached in safety-leaving M'Donald in the quiet possession of the castle he had been striving to capture in vain. Some two or three of M'Donald's Indians lingered about the premises to ascertain the fate of their leader; and finding that Shell and his family had evacuated the post, ventured in to visit him. Not being able to remove him; however, on taking themselves off, they charged their wounded leader to inform Shell, that if he would be kind to him, (M'Donald,) they would take good care of his (Shell's) captive boys. M'Donald was the next day removed to the fort by Captain Small, where his leg was amputated; but the blood could not be stanched, and he died in a few hours.+ The lads were carried into Canada. The loss of the enemy on the ground was eleven killed and six wounded. The boys, who were rescued after the war, reported that they took twelve of their wounded away with them, nine of whom died before they arrived in Canada.++

At a subsequent day, Shell, being at work in the field with his two sons at no great distance from the fort, was fired upon by a party of Indians concealed in the standing wheat, and

* One of Shell's neighbors lay in ambush during the battle, and heard Shell's directions to Small and Getman.
+ M'Donald wore a silver-mounted tomahawk, which was taken from him by Shell. It was marked by thirty scalp-notches, showing that few Indians could have been more industrious than himself in gathering that description of military trophies.
++ Among the slain was a white man, who had two thumbs on one hand. One of Shell's sons is yet living in Canada, being a member of the Dunkard's Society, in the neighborhood of Toronto.

severely wounded. He called to his sons not to allow the Indians to scalp him ; and neither of the brave boys would retreat until a guard came from the fort to their relief. But in the discharge of this filial duty, one of them was killed and the other wounded. John Christian Shell himself died of his wound, in the fort. His deeds were commemorated in one of the most rude and prosaic of ballads. But his memory is yet green in the remembrance of the German population of Herkimer.*

The policy of the enemy at the north, during the whole season, was to divide their own forces into small detachments, and harass the border settlements at as many different points as possible-thus distracting the attention of the people, and by allowing them neither a sense of security nor repose, rendering them disgusted with the protracted struggle. The most formidable movement of the Indians and Tories during the Summer months, was the descent of Captain Cauldwell, from Niagara, upon the border of Ulster County, at the head of about four hundred Indians and Tories. The first intelligence of this irruption was received in Albany by General Gansevoort,+ by letter, as follows:-

GOVERNOR CLINTON TO GENERAL GANSEVOORT.
"Poughkeepsie, August 14, 1781
"SIR,

"Last Sunday, a body of the enemy, to the amount of about three hundred Indians and ninety Tories, appeared on the frontiers of Ulster County. They took a small scout Colonel Pauling

---

* This account of John Christian Shell's exploit has been drawn chiefly from the MS. statement of the venerable Col. William Feeter, yet living in that town, [Feb. 1838,] and from the ballad mentioned in the text, which contains a pathetic and particular recitation of the facts. This use of contemporaneous ballads as authority for facts is well sustained by precedent. Thierry makes bold use of English Norman ballads for his history of the Norman Conquest; and Prescott, in his late invaluable history of the reigns of Ferdinand and Isabella, has done the like with the ancient Castilian romance and Moorish ballad.

+ In the re-organization of the army, at the close of the year 1780, Colonel Gansevoort was left out of service in the line, by seniority in rank of other officers. Being a brigadier general of the militia, however, stationed at Albany, his services were in continual requisition, since, in the absence of regular troops, his brigade was the chief dependence of the northern section of the State. His activity in the State service was incessant, and his correspondence with the Governor and the general officers of the regular army at the north, heavier than at any former period.

---

had sent out, and from them it is supposed obtained information of the disposition of the levies in that quarter, whom they passed by, and -were first discovered at the settlement of Warwasing. From the last accounts they had retired; but how far, is not known. The militia have been collected and marched to oppose or pursue them, as circumstances may render expedient. From their force, it is not probable they will leave the country without attempting farther mischief in that or some other quarter. I conceive it necessary, therefore, to give you this information that you may take proper steps with your militia in case this party should take their route toward the frontier of your county; and I would particularly recommend that a part of your brigade be immediately marched to Schoharie, for the protection of that settlement until this party shall entirely have gone off. The account of the enemy's strength is from one Vrooman, who deserted them; which is confirmed from their appearance to a small party of levies, who saw them paraded at a house they attacked, and which the party defended. By a more particular account received this morning, (and which was the first that demanded credit,) they have burnt and destroyed about a dozen houses, with their barns, &c., among which are those of John G. Hardenburgh, Esq. They killed only one of the inhabitants, the rest having made a timely escape from their houses. The levies stationed there were by no means sufficient to turn out and oppose them; but those who were in the house defended themselves with spirit against the assaults of the enemy, by which means several of them are said to have fallen, and many houses were saved.

"I am, with great esteem,

"Sir, your most obd't serv't,

"GEO. CLINTON.

"Brig. Gen. Gansevoort."*

Captain Cauldwell was an officer in Butler's rangers. Who

* Colonel Vrooman, at Schoharie, having heard of the invasion of Ulster County by Cauldwell, wrote a pressing letter to General Gansevoort, for assistance, on the same day that the Governor wrote from Poughkeepsie. Colonel Henry Van Rensselaer was forthwith ordered to Schoharie with his regiment, and Colonel Wemple was directed to send a detachment of his regiment thither, from Schenectady, together with as many of the Oneida Indians as he could engage. Fortunately, their services were not required in action.

was the Indian leader on the occasion, is not known. Their route from Niagara had been by way of the Chemung, and thence, after crossing the Susquehanna, by the Lackawaxen to the Delaware. The stockade forts at the north of the Lackawaxen, and at Neversink, had been passed unobserved. Luckily, however, for the inhabitants, shortly before Cauldwell reached the settlements, a scouting party had descried his advance, and, eluding the enemy's pursuit, had succeeded in communicating the alarm to the people, who at once fled with their most valuable effects to the picket forts erected for exactly such emergencies.

It was just at the first blush of morning that Cauldwell passed the small fortress on the frontier of Warwasing. Being fired upon by the sentinel, the report alarmed Captain Hardenburgh, who, with a guard of nine men, was stationed at a point about three miles distant from the fort. Proceeding immediately in the direction of the sound, Hardenburgh and his little band met the enemy on his way, directing their course toward the adjoining settlement of Mombackus-now called Rochester.

Nothing daunted, the Captain gave the enemy battle; but being closely pressed, he soon discovered that his retreat had been cut off by a party of Indians, who had gained his rear. In this dilemma, it being yet not quite light, Hardenburgh with his party took refuge in a small stone house near by, owned by a Mr. Kettle, which had probably not been observed by the enemy Here they found six militia-men more-making sixteen in all, and being well armed, they gave the invaders a warm reception The latter advanced several times to carry the house by assault, but as some of their number were each time doomed to fall, they as often gave way, and in the end relinquished the undertaking- leaving thirteen dead upon the field. In marching forward two miles to Hardenburgh's house, the enemy fell in with Kettle, the owner of the premises where they had been so roughly handled. He, poor fellow, was killed and scalped.*

Captain Henry Pauling, with a detachment of the regiment of State levies commanded by Colonel Albert Pauling, was stationed at a point about six miles distant from the scene of the action just described. He hastened forward, but arrived too

*MS. Statement of Captain Valentine Davis, in the author's possession.

late to have a brush with the enemy, and only in season to capture one strangling prisoner who was lingering for fruit in an apple orchard.* Finding his reception rather warm, and perceiving indications of farther and more powerful opposition to his advance, Cauldwell was already in full retreat. Nor did he commence retracing his steps a moment too soon for his own safety. The news of his advance having reached the west bank of the Hudson, where Colonel Pauling, of the State levies; and Colonel John Cantine, with a body of militia, were stationed, those officers marched immediately to the relief of the invaded settlements.

They arrived at the outskirts in time to catch a glimpse of the enemy's rear, and to relieve some of the inhabitants, among whom were a man and his -wife, who had conducted themselves with distinguished bravery. His house was constructed of unhewn logs, in the woods, and in advance of all others. On the appearance of the foe, he fled to his castle with his wife, and securing it in the best manner he could, gave battle to a party of the Indians who laid siege to his fortress. Being well armed, he defended himself with so much spirit, that they recoiled with loss. Finding, after several attempts, that they could not force an entrance, the Indians collected a heap of combustibles, and set fire to the premises.

Retiring a short distance to see the result, the man watched his opportunity, and rushing out with a couple of buckets, he procured water, which was close at hand, and extinguished the fire. The Indians, of course, ran down upon him; but not being quick enough of foot to prevent his gaining the door, hurled their tomahawks at his head-happily without effect. He entered his castle, made fast his sally-port, and re-commenced his defence. Just at this moment Colonel Pauling with his troops appeared in sight, whereupon the Indians raised the siege and departed. Colonel Pauling was absent in pursuit seven days, but did not overtake them. The enemy suffered severely. They lost a goodly number of their men; took only two prisoners and but little plunder; and were so near starvation, that they were compelled to devour their dogs before they reached their head-quarters.-+

*MS. of Major Thomas Sammons, who was at this time serving in the corps of Captain Pauling. The prisoner taken from the enemy was recognized as an old neighbor of his father's at Johnstown, who had served in the company of which Jacob Sammons was the lieutenant. +Major Sammons.

The Shawanese and other western Indians seem to have remained comparatively quiet during the Spring and Summer of 1781. The Kentucky settlements were for the most part unmolested, save by a feeble attack upon M'Afee's station near Harrodsburgh. The assailants, however, were but a straggling party of Indians, who hung about the stockade, and were ultimately punished severely for their temerity. Two of them were killed by an equal number of the M'Afees, whom, having left the fort for some purpose, the Indians attempted to cut off on their return. The Indians then commenced an attack upon the fort, but a party of cavalry arriving suddenly from Harrodsburgh, the garrison sallied forth, and the savages were quickly dispersed, with a loss of six killed outright, and several others, whom they bore away, wounded. A few days afterward, Bryant's station, which was yet more exposed, was visited by the Indians. Bryant, who was a brother-in-law of Colonel Boon, having arranged a large hunting party of twenty men, left his fort on an expedition down the Elk-horn. Having divided his company in order to sweep a broader extent of country for game, by reason of a fog, and other untoward circumstances, they failed of uniting at the points designated. Meantime the Indians were hanging about both divisions, and by stratagem succeeded in defeating both. In one of their skirmishes Bryant was mortally wounded, and another man severely. It was reported that the hunters, taken by surprise, were deficient in firmness, when Bryant fell. On the following day they encountered the Indians again, and defeated them.

Willett's ill-fated expedition to Oswego, and reason for failure.

Oswego Expedition

Fort Herkimer 19 February 1783
Sir.

It is no small mortification to me, to have occasion to report to your Excellency that our Expedition to Oswego has not been successful--Nothing could be more pleasing than our prospect was, when we were within four or five miles of Oswego between ten and eleven o'clock on the night of the 12th instant, with every thing ready to make the attack--but our expectations were blasted by a very unexpected event, and event which I had not the least reason to apprehend, considering the pains I had taken to prevent such a contingency from taking place—The caution your Excellency had given me respecting guides, had made me doubly careful in procuring such as I conceived would most assuredly preserve me from danger from want of good pilots—I had provided myself with four persons who deserted from Oswego since the beginning of last August—I had several men with me who were well acquainted with Oswego, and were otherwise intelligent & smart—besides which, I took with the three Oneida Indians, all of high estimation with respect to their fidelity, and one in particular, called Captain John, who has a commission from Congress, whose behavior has been uniformly upright in all the changes of our affairs, and who is a very expert Indian—yet, notwithstanding this, it was my guide that ruined me.

On my arrival at the West end of the Oneida Lake, I found the sleighs to be an incumberance, and that they increased the danger of our being discovered—for this reason it was determined to leave them at that place, and march the remainder of the way thro the woods—In little better than a days march we got below Oswego falls, twelve mile only from Oswego, not far from that place, I ventured to have our Ladders made, and at eight o'clock in the evening we left the woods, and went on the ice three miles below the falls—We proceeded cautiously on the ice until we arrived at a point about four miles from Oswego here the ice failing, we were obliged to go on shore and enter the woods—

The guides had uniformly submitted their judgment the whole of the way to the superior knowledge of Captain John, and he still continued to go on in front marking out our rout—thus far he had led us well, land he now told me he would bring us by midnight into a road made to haul wood to the Fort, not more than two miles from the Garrison, and that it was not more than two miles to that road, so that our whole march was not to exceed four miles and it was not then quite eleven o'clock.

This information produced fresh ardour in every breast, every countenance brightened and the ladders, which in any other case would have been an intolerable incumbrance, moved lightly thro the woods.—Deep snow, high hills of deep morasses were passed with briskness & cheerfulness that was truly pleasing until after following him near three hours without observing any signs of the Fort and by our zigzag movements it appeared evident that our course was not right.

I was considerably advanced in front following close after the guide on snow shoes when these suspicions entered fully into my mind, both from the irregularity of his course as well as the length of time we had been marching without arriving at the Fort.—In declaring my suspicious to my Guides, they all appeared entirely lost—In this situation I was compelled to halt the Troops while I endeavored myself, and by sending others in different routs, to find the way to the fort—but it was all in vain. The Moon had set and the day was dawning, when I was out with two of the best hands I had, endeavouring to discover our way without effecting it—Thus were our expectations, which but a few hours before were raised to the highest pitch from a persuasion that we were almost in sight of the Fort in the most silent hour of the night without being discovered, blasted by the unaccountable conduct of our Guide—surmises were made that Captain John the Indian led us wrong designedly, this however is a surmise that I cannot give into—his former conduct has been regular and good, and I had given him such expectation in case of success, as will not admit of the supposition of his having willfully taken measures to disappoint us—

I am inclined to think that the cause of his losing the way was this –soon after he left the ice he came on a snow shoe track, which he followed a considerable way supposing it would lead to the Fort and that after finding he had been led into an error and wasted much time he got bewildered—his behaviour however had a bad appearance, which occasioned my ordering him under guard together with the other two Indians his companions.—

As long as there was a prospect of affecting the business of the expedition no Troops could exhibit a more cheerfull fortitude under the severest task than did the whole of the officers of soldiers, but as that prospect vanished with the approaching day, their great fatigue got the better of the spirits of the soldiers, land as we could have no right to hope to remain several small parties of the enemy made their appearance on the opposite shore, and some few miles higher up, three Seneca Indians came to us with professions of Friendship—as they put themselves in our power, and made a friendly appearance, I did not think it proper to do any thing with them, but preferred them to stand & see the troops march by at a distance, & bid them farewell.

Thus, Sir, I have reported to your Excellency the progress and unfortunate issue of this business—a business in which I had promised myself much satisfaction, as well in rendering service to my Country, as in achieving fame for the officers and soldiers employed in executing it—Providence has ordered it otherwise.

I cannot help feeling great regret at the disappointment, whilst I reflect with gratitude on the honor conferred on me by your Excellency in affording me an opportunity of acquiring so much as so small a risk.—I pretend not that the work has been performed as well as it might have been, perhaps I have been deficient in point of [discomment?], but I am sure I have not been in points of exertion, these have been stretched to their utmost, yet I have unfortunately failed—failed at a time when I looked on the prize just ready to fall into my hands, which was truly the case from ten to one o'clock on the of the twelfth Instant, with every thing ready to made the attack we were just within view of the fort undiscovered, while every breast was filled with ardor and the most animated determination—but lost it in the strange and unaccountable manner I have related.

I have the honor to be, with the most profound respect and esteem

Sir Your Excellency's most obed't and very hum servant.
Marinus Willett.
His Excellency
Genl Washington

FROM: The Papers of the Continental Congress. 8 pages. Item Number 152, Publication Number: M247. Letters from Gen. George Washington, Commander in Chief of the Army, 1775-84; June 16, 1775-Sept 18, 1776 (Vols 1-11) Ltrs. from Gen. George Washington Volume 11. Date 19 Feb. 1783 Roll Number 171.

The Frontiersmen of New York
by Jeptha R. Simms
Albany, NY 1883
Volume II, Page 645.
PRINCIPAL EVENTS OF 1783.

An Abortive Attempt of Col. Willett to Capture Fort Oswego.
- Said *Moses Nelson*, an American prisoner there in the spring of 1782, when the enemy set about rebuilding Fort Oswego, three officers, Capt. Nellis, Lieut. James Hare, and Ensign Robert Nellis, a son of the Captain, all of the forester service, had charge of the Indians there, employed. Nelson and two other lads, also prisoners, accompanied this party, which was conveyed in a sloop, as waiters. About 100 persons were employed in rebuilding this fortress, which occupied most of the season. The winter following, Nelson remained at this fort and was in it when Col. Willett advanced with a body of troops February 9, 1783, with the intention of taking it by surprise. The enterprise is said to have proved abortive in consequence of Col. Willett's guide, who was an Oneida Indian, having lost his way in the night when within only a few miles of the fort. The men were illy provided for their return-certain victory having been anticipated-and their sufferings were, in consequence, very severe. This enterprise was undertaken agreeably to the orders of Gen. Washington; but it certainly added no laurels to the chaplet of the brave Willett.

After the above was first published, I learned from John Roof, who was a private soldier in that enterprise under Willett, that so certain did the latter feel of success, that a scant quantity of provisions were taken along. While on the way out, several dogs with the army were killed to prevent betraying their position, which the famished troops were glad on their homeward march to dig out of the snow and eat.

Col. Willett, possibly, may not have known, as well as Washington did, that Fort Oswego had been so strongly fitted up the preceding year, and consequently the difficulties he had to encounter before its capture-be that as it may, the probability is, that had the attack been made, the impossibility of scaling the walls would have frustrated the design, with the loss of many brave men. The fort was surrounded by a deep moat, in which were planted heavy pickets. From the lower part of the walls projected downward and outward another row of pickets. A draw-bridge enabled the inmates to pass out and in, which was drawn up and secured, to the wall every night, and the corners were built out so that mounted cannon commanded the trenches. Two of Willett's men, badly frozen, entered the fort in the morning, surrendering themselves prisoners, from whom the garrison learned the object of the enterprise.

The ladders prepared by Willett to scale the walls were left on his return, and a party of British soldiers went and brought them in. The longest of them," said Nelson," when placed against the walls inside the pickets,- reached only about two-thirds of the way to the top." The post was strongly garrisoned, and it was the opinion of Mr. N. that the accident or treachery which misled the troops was most providential, tending to save Col. Willett from defeat, and most of his men from certain death.

Gen. Washington reported the failure of this enterprise to the President of Congress, February 25, 1783, as follows:

" SIR-I am sorry to acquaint your Excellency-for the information of Congress-that a project which I had formed, for attacking the enemy's fort at Oswego-as soon as the sleighing should be good, and the ice of the Oneida lake should have acquired sufficient thickness to admit the passage of a detachment-has miscarried. The report of Col. Willett, to whom I had entrusted the command of the party, consisting of a part of the Rhode Island regiment and the State troops of New York-in all about 500 men-will assign reasons for the disappointment."

He added that, although the expedition had failed, "I am certain nothing depended upon Col. Willett to give efficiency to it, was wanting."-*Sparks' Life of Washington*, vol. 8, p. 385.

How the Forerunner of Peace, a Notice of the Cessation of Hostilities Between Great Britain and the United States, was sent from Fort Plain to Fort Oswego.-

In July, 1880, Rev. Dr. Denis Wortman placed in my hands a journal of Capt. Alexander Thompson,* an officer in the American artillery service, which journal now belongs to the family of Thomas T. Buckley, Esq., of Brooklyn, N. Y.-Mrs. B. being a sister of Rev. Dr. Alex. R. Thompson, the third of the name-the second, Col. A. R. Thompson, having been killed in the Florida war. The journal, which consists of 50-five and a half by seven and a half-well written pages, has the following heading:

"JOURNAL of a tour from the AMERICAN GARRISON at Fort Rensselaer, in Canajoharie, on the Mohawk River, to the BRITISH GARRISON of OSWEGO, as a Flagg, to announce a cessation of hostilities on the frontiers of New York, commenced. Friday, April 18, 1783."

On the first of January of this year, Capt. Thompson, as his journal shows, was appointed to the artillery command of several posts of the Mohawk valley, which he names as follows: Fort Rensselaer, Fort Plank, Fort Herkimer

---

* A native of East Windsor, Ct. He with William Burns, of Coventry, and Charles Brown, all of Connecticut, are said to have been the first three of the forlorn hope to enter the enemy's works at Stoney Point, under the impetuous Gen. Wayne.

---

and Fort Dayton. Fort Rensselaer*-another name for Fort Plain-being, as he says, the headquarters of the river forts, he thought proper to have his own quarters near those of the commanding officer, so as to furnish from his own company detachments, as circumstances required. On the 17th of April-only a little over two months after Col. Willett's attempt to surprise Fort Oswego-an express arrived at Fort Plain from Washington's headquarters, to have an officer sent from thence with a flag to Oswego, to announce to that garrison-from whence many of the Indian depredators came-a general cessation of hostilities, and an impending peace.

Maj. Andrew Finck, then in command at Fort Plain, committed this important and hazardous mission to Capt. Thompson. His companions in the enterprise were to be four, a bombardier of his own company, a sergeant of Willett's levies, and a Stockbridge Indian, and his guide and interpreter was to join him at Fort Herkimer. We regret that he did not give the names of his attendants. All things were to be ready for an early start on the morning of the 18th, but when the nature of his mission became known along the valley-and such news as he was bearer of sped on fleet horses-many having lost friends whose fate was unknown, desired a chance to send letters by the flag bearer, and his start was thus delayed until 11 o'clock, at which hour numerous small packets and letters were collected to be sent to friends in Canada. To some inquiries, he said on his return, his mission proved one of joy, but to others one of sadness; as the veil of mysteries had not been lifted. A flag of truce having been made by securing a white cloth to the head of a spittoon, to be borne by the sergeant, he left the fort with the flag-man in front of him, and the artillery-man and Indian in his rear. He started with a pack-horse, which he discreetly left at Fort Herkimer. The novelty of his mission drew a great crowd together, and he was accompanied several miles by a cavalcade of officers, soldiers and citizens. He went up the

---

* It is much to be deprecated that Gen. Van Rensselaer, in pursuit of Sir John Johnson in the fall of 1780, after this fort had been known on the frontier by no other name than that of Fort plain for four years, should have taken the liberty to change its name to his own. This is worse than calling Fort Stanwix Fort Schuyler, because that was, though very unwisely, so done at the beginning of the war. Col. Willett, although in command of Fort Plain when its name was purloined, we thought could not have advised so unwise a measure, but he connived at it. Would any one expect a Patroon, to have presumed on such an act?

---

river road on the south side of the Mohawk, and spoke of passing Fort Windecker (now Mindenville), and the Canajoharie, or Upper Mohawk castle (now Danube where the Mohawk's church still stands), arriving at Mr. Schuyler's house at the foot of Fall Hill, about 3 o'clock p. M., where he and his party were presented with an excellent dinner. This halt was but a little distance from the Gen. Herkimer house, which is still standing. I suppose this Schuyler to have been keeping a public house where Warner Dygert was residing, when killed by the Indians several years before. Leaving Schuyler's at 4 P. M., he passed over Fall Hill and arrived at Fort Herkimer after sunset.

At this garrison Capt. Thompson found David Schuyler, a brother of the man he had dined with, who became his guide and interpreter. Eight days rations were put into knapsacks, and one short musket was concealed in a blanket, with which to kill game, if by any means their provisions failed. On Saturday morning, April 19, in a snow storm, this party of five set out on their wilderness journey, still on the south side of the Mohawk.

They met several hunting parties, and made their first halt opposite "Thompson's place above New Germantown", now in the town of Schuyler. A few miles above he fell in with a party of 10 families of Indians on a hunting excursion, and learned how forest children lived, and after passing through a swampy defile, he encamped on solid ground for the night Here his men instructed by the Indian soon erected an Indian wigwam for the night, in the following manner:

Two stakes, with crotches at the upper end, were set upright about 10 feet apart, upon which they placed a pole. They then covered the sides with bark resting the top against the pole with the bottom on the ground, so as to leave a space about 12 feet wide. The gables were also covered with bark; a fire was made in the middle of the structure, and a small hole left in the top for smoke to pass out, and when some hemlock boughs had been cut for their beds, the tabernacle was completed.

Such a structure the Indians would construct in an incredible space of time, where bark was handily obtained. In such rude huts, many a hunter or weary traveler has found a good night's rest.

The next morning the journey was resumed on the Fort Stanwix road, and at 10 o'clock he passed the ruins of old Fort Schuyler, of the French war, now Utica. On Capt. Thompson's arrival at the "Seekaquate" creek-Sadaquada or Saquoit creek which enters the Mohawk at Whitestown-he found the bridge gone. Soon after passing this stream he said he ascended "Ariska (Oriskany) Hill," which he observed "was usually allowed to be the highest piece of ground from Schenectada to Fort Stanwix."

Says the journal: "I went over the ground where Gen. Herkimer fought Sir John Johnson, this is allowed to be one of the most desperate engagements that has ever been fought by the militia. I saw a vast number of human skulls and bones scattered through the woods;" this was nearly five and a half years after the battle. He halted to view the ruins of Fort Stanwix, and those of St. Ledger's works while besieging the fort, and passing the sight of Fort Bull on Wood creek, at the end of a mile and a half he encamped for the night, erecting the usual Indian wigwam.

The night was one of terror, as the howling of wolves and other animals prevented much sleep, but keeping up their fires the beasts were kept at bay. Monday morning, on arriving at Canada creek, a tributary to Wood creek, two trees were felled to bridge the stream. A mile and a half below he left the creek and ascended Pine ridge, where he discovered in his path a human foot-print made by a shoe, which indicated a white wearer. On arriving at Fish creek he halted to fish, but with poor success.

He had purposed to cross the creek and pursue his way to Oswego on the north side of Oneida lake, striking Oswego river near the falls, but learning from his Indian, who had recently been on a scout to the Three Rivers, that he had seen three flat bottomed boats with oars, as the ice had but recently left the lakes and thinking they might still be there, he changed his course for Wood creek, and striking it at a well known place called the "Scow," he had a raft made and sent the Indian and sergeant to search for the boats in Oneida creek, and to return the same evening.

The three remaining at the Scow were soon searching for material for a cabin, but neither bark or hemlock could be found, and as it was fast growing dark, they collected what logs and wood they could to keep up a good fire, which was started. At 8 o'clock it began to rain terribly, and in two or three hours, their fire was put out. As the boat seekers did not come back that night, it became one of great anxiety and discontent. The men returned after day-light, and reported a serviceable boat without oars, which they had launched and towed round the edge of the lake and left at the Royal Block House, known as Fort Royal, at the mouth of Wood creek. No time was lost in reaching the boat, which was found to leak badly. They caulked it as best they could with an old rope. From a board oars were soon made, a pole raised and blankets substituted for a sale with bark billiards; and, having everything on board, they moved into Oneida lake-20 miles long with a favorable but light wind. It was deemed prudent with their craft to run across the lake to Nine Mile Point, on the north shore, but before reaching it, two men were kept constantly bailing. The boat was again repaired and put afloat, sailing from point to point. As night approached, the crew landed about half way down the lake, where they improvised a cabin, with a good fire to dry their clothes. The night was pleasant, but the howling of wild beasts was again terrific.

On Wednesday, the 23d, a beautiful day, the party were early on the move, and from the middle of the lake Capt. Thompson said he could see both ends of it, and enjoyed one of the most delightful views imaginable. There were several islands on the western side of the lake covered with lofty timber, while back of the Oneida castles, he said, the elevated grounds made a very beautiful prospect.

After about eight miles sail, he heard a gun, evidently fired by an enemy; but, to avoid observation, he sailed along the shore until he was opposite the Six Mile Islands-as the two largest islands in the "lake, lying side by side, are called-when he went ashore, where a fire was kindled and a good dinner enjoyed ; after which he again dropped down the lake, passed Fort Brewerton, at the east end of the lake, and entered the Oneida river. Here he found a rapid current in his favor, and the river the most serpentine of any stream he had ever been on, abounding, at that season, with immense quantities of wild fowl, especially of ducks in many varieties. He saw many flocks of geese, but he would not allow the old musket to be fired, lest a lurking scout might be attracted to his position. He continued his course down the river, sometimes on the Onondaga side, and at others on the Oswego side.

A Change in the Programme.-About two miles from Three Rivers-nearly 20 miles from Oneida lake-he discovered a party of Indians in three canoes, coming up the river on the same shore. On seeing his boat they gave a yell, and paddled to the opposite shore. His white flag was planted on the bow of the boat, but they did not at first distinguish it, and, supposing the boat contained a hostile party, they landed, drew their canoes out of the water, ascended the bank and took to trees.

When the flag was opposite, they hailed in Indian and in English, which last was answered. When assured that the Captain had a flag of truce, the Canadians asked him to come ashore. Four Indians then came out from behind trees, and beckoned to him to land: he did so, and was conducted into the woods. His men also landed, and the Indians drew his boat well on shore. He was conducted to the presence of two white men and an old Indian, who were seated on the ground. One of them told

Capt. Thompson his name was Hare, a Lieutenant of Butler's rangers, and had just started on an enterprise to the neighborhood of Fort Plain.

He assured the Lieutenant that all hostilities had ceased on the war path, and that his mission was to convey such intelligence to the commanding officer of Fort Oswego. Lieut. Hare seemed much surprised, and said no such news had been received there. When assured the American scouts had all been called in, after several consultations the war party-consisting of one other white man and eight Indians, all being painted alike-concluded to take him to the fort, saying if the measure proved a. finesse, they had him sure. He was conducted back to his boat to the great relief of his friends, who were exercised by thoughts of treachery; and with a canoe on each side of the boat, and one behind it, the flotilla passed down the river, the Lieutenant taking a seat with Captain T. in his boat. The party glided down past the Three Rivers-Three Rivers point is formed by the junction of the Oneida and Seneca rivers, forming the third on Oswego river-about six miles below which they landed and encamped for the night, constructing two cabins, one of which Lieut. Hare, Capt. Thompson and two Indians occupied, the remainder of both parties using the other. The Oswego river is 24 miles long.

Early on Thursday morning, Lieut. Hare sent one of his canoes to Oswego, to inform the commander of the approaching flag; and soon after sunrise they all embarked down the rapids, which increased as they approached the Falls. On arriving there they drew the boat around the carrying place, and safely passing the rifts below, they stopped within a mile of Lake Ontario, where they were bailed by a sentinel on shore, to await orders from the commandant of the fort.

At the end of an hour, Lieut. McLane, of the eighth regiment received him, to whom he presented his instructions, which pointedly required his delivery of them to the commanding officer of the garrison. McLane wanted to send the dispatches by another officer; to this the Captain would not consent, and he had to wait further instructions. In a short time Mr. Frazier, Lieutenant and Adjutant of the garrison, arrived with Maj. Ross's compliments to conduct him to the fort, which he did blind folded; and taking Frazier's arm he thus entered the fortress. He heard the draw-bridge over the trench let down-the chains of which made a remarkable clattering. He was conducted up a flight of steps and into a room where the handkerchief was removed from his eyes, and he was presented by the Adjutant to Maj. Ross, the commanding officer, who received him very courteously, and to whom he delivered his instructions and dispatches; and who told him to be seated and partake of provided refreshments, such as cold ham, fowl, wine, etc., while he perused the papers. That the traveler did justice to the collation we cannot doubt.

Maj. Ross told his guest he had brought very different intelligence from that which he had received recently from Gov. Haldimand, and added that 14 days before he had received orders from Quebec, to prepare his post with every exertion for its defense against an expected invasion of the Americans at the beginning of May, and that lie would be obliged to continue the working parties, and forward the dispatches to Gen. McLane, at Niagara-pledging his honor that all his own scouts should at once be called home. He ordered the Sloop Caldwell, mounting 14 guns and then lying near the fort, to sail immediately to that garrison with the dispatches.

Before his arrival and the nature of the Captain's mission was known, curtains were put to the windows looking out upon the lake, but they were now removed, and Maj. Ross asked his guest to look out and see the Caldwell take her departure for Fort Niagara. The view from the window in the sun-light upon the wide waters of the lake was a delightful one.

Maj. Ross took occasion to inform the Captain in a delicate and polite manner; that although he had brought the first news of approaching peace, but that his garrison consisted of different corps of troops, on which account he was not at liberty to show him the situation of Oswego with its improved fortifications, for which be hoped full allowance would be made. In a letter subsequently sent the Captain at Fort Rensselaer-Fort Plain-the Major further explained why he could not be as complaisant and commutative to him when at Fort Oswego, as his inclination or better nature prompted.

After Maj. Ross had expressed his delicate situation to his guest, the latter presented him the letters and descriptions of prisoners made in Central New York, which he agreed should be promptly attended to. He said it was impossible for any officer to control the savages when on excursions, and he really believed that many cruel depredations had been committed by them on our frontiers, known only to themselves. He said he had exerted himself to prevent the murdering of any prisoners, "but the utmost effort," said he, "could not prevent them from taking the scalps of the killed." He must have known that the Indian's desire to obtain scalps, was to receive for them the proffered bounty offered by the government which he served. The Major took occasion to say that he was very happy that such an unnatural war was at an end: saying, however, that war created the Soldier's Harvest. Maj. Ross was one of the most successful, as well as humane invaders of Central New York.

Nothing, said Capt. Thompson, seemed to affect Maj. Ross so much as did the published articles of peace by both nations, naming the boundaries of the United States. He got out maps and began to traverse the lines, only to find that the posts of Oswego, Niagara and Detroit, had all been ceded to the United States; and still more was he mortified to learn that they were all to be surrendered in their present condition.

But he controlled his feelings as best he could. He introduced a number of officers to the Captain, who, said the latter were all civil except Capt. Crawford, who had joined the

British standard, when the enemy took New York city in 1776, and who now belonged to Sir John Johnson's Greens. "This person," said the Captain, "comes under that despicable character of a loyal subject. He appeared to be really ignorant of the cause he was fighting for, and had the wickedness to observe that he had made more money in the British service in the war, than he would have made in the American service in a hundred years. Capt. T. gave him to understand that American officers were engaged in the service from principle, and not for money. Maj. Ross and the other officers were disposed to treat the flag bearer courteously, and Crawford was obliged to choke down his politics, and offer a lame apology. The Captain took as little notice of this violent partisan as possible, during the rest of his stay.

Maj. Ross invited Capt. Thompson to remain a few days longer, and said that he would send his own barge with him up the rivers, lake and Wood creek; he expressed his thanks and said he wished to return on the west side of the river, as that would take him through a country he had not explored. The Major said he should manifest his pleasure, but he would be happy to afford him any assistance. On Saturday the Major told him that the Indians had been clamorous, some one having told them that all their lands were to be taken from them, and they were to be driven to where the sun went down. He had also learned from some source that they had threatened his life on his return, and said it was necessary he should know it: he also assured him that lie would take every measure to prevent insult or injury, for which purpose he would send a detachment of troops to protect him as near his own garrison as he might think proper.

Capt. Thompson suggested leaving the next morning, and Maj. Ross required Adj't Ferguson to make a list of the persons he presented the names of, that he might report whether they were still alive or not. This list was given him in the evening. He then learned that a lad 14 years old was there a prisoner, who had been captured near Fort Dayton, and at the Captain's request, the boy, who was incapable of bearing arms-was allowed to return with him to his anxious parents. It is a pity the boy's name was not mentioned. He was a feeling lad, and was very grateful for the intercession of the Captain in his behalf. Thanking Maj. Ross for his kind entertainment, he was again blind folded, and taking the arms of Adj't Ferguson and Lieut. Hare, he was conducted without the fort and to his attendants in the mission at his boat at 11 o'clock P. M., on Sunday the 27th. The journal here ends abruptly, and the presumption is, that the balance of his memoranda was put into another small book-which may or may not be yet extant. As Maj. Ross agreed to have an escort ready to protect him on the journey back from savage insult, he no doubt sent a detachment of troops with him for some distance, perhaps under one of the officers named. In due time he again safely reached Fort Plain. Thus have we been able to present, at the end of nearly a century, the first published account of this important event in the annals of border-warfare.

Washington's Newburgh Headquarters. Washington in the Mohawk Valley.-In the spring of 1783, an order for the cessation of hostilities between Great Britain and the United States, was published in the camp of the latter just eight years after the battle of Lexington, but an army organization was kept up until fall. As the initiatory step to his contemplated tour of observation in Central New York, Gen. Washington wrote to Gen. Philip Schuyler, from his Newburgh Headquarters, July 15, 1783, as follows:

"DEAR SIR-I have always entertained a great desire to see the northern part of this State, before I returned Southward. The present irksome interval, while we are waiting for the definitive treaty, affords an opportunity of gratifying this inclination. I have therefore concerted with Geo. Clinton to make a tour to reconnoiter those places, where the most remarkable posts were established, and the ground which became famous by being the theatre of action in 1777. On our return from thence, we propose to pass across the Mohawk river, in order to have a view of that tract of country, which is so much celebrated for the fertility of its soil and the beauty of its situation. We shall set out by water on Friday the 18th, if nothing shall intervene to prevent our journey.

"Mr. Dimler, assistant quartermaster-general, who will have the honor of delivering this letter, precedes us to make arrangements, and particularly to have some light boats provided and transported to Lake George, that we may not be delayed on arrival there.

"I pray you, my dear sir, to be so good as to advise Mr. Dimler in what manner to proceed in this business, to excuse the trouble I am about to give you, and to be persuaded that your kind information and direction to the bearer will greatly increase the obligations, with which I have the honor to be, etc."-*Sparks Life*, 8, 425.

July 16th Washington wrote to the President of Congress as follows:

"Finding myself in most disagreeable circumstances here, and likely to be, so long as Congress are pleased to continue me in this awkward situation, anxiously expecting the definitive treaty; without command, and with little else to do, than to be teased with troublesome applications and fruitless demands, which I have neither the means nor the power of satisfaction: in this distressing tedium I have resolved to wear away a little time in performing a tour to the northward, as far as Ticonderoga and Crown Point, and perhaps as far up the Mohawk river as Fort Schuyler. I shall leave this place (Newburgh) on Friday next, and shall probably be gone about two weeks, unless my tour should be interrupted by some special recall. One gentleman of my family will be left here to receive any letters or commands that shall be necessary."-*Sparks*.

Washington got back to his headquarters, August 5th, and the next day he wrote to the President of Congress. After speaking of his return, which was by water from Albany to Newburgh, he says:

"My tour having been extended as far northward as Crown Point, and westward to Fort Schuyler (Stanwix) and its district, and my movements having been pretty rapid, my horses, which are not yet arrived, will be so much fatigued, that they will need some days to recruit, etc."

In another letter of the same date he renews the subject, and says: "I was the more particularly induced by two considerations to make the tour, which in my letter of the 16th ultimo, I informed Congress I had in contemplation, and from which I returned last evening. The one was an inclination to see the northern and western posts of this State, with those places which have been the theatre of important military transactions; the other a desire to facilitate, as far in my power, the operations, which will be necessary for occupying the posts which are ceded by the treaty of peace, as soon as they shall be evacuated by the British troops."

He had his eye upon Detroit as a point to be looked after, and wanted some of the well affected citizens of that place to preserve the fortifications and public buildings there, "until such time as a garrison could be sent with provisions and stores sufficient to take and hold possession of them. The propriety of this measure has appeared in a more forcible point of light, since I have been up the Mohawk river, and taken a view of the situation of things in that quarter, etc." Elsewhere he adds: "I engaged at Fort Rensselaer,* a gentleman whose name is Cassaty, formerly a resident at Detroit, and who is well recommended, to proceed without loss of time, find out the disposition of the inhabitants, and make every previous inquiry, which might be necessary for the information of the Baron on his arrival, that he should be able to make such final arrangements, as the circumstances might appear to justify. This seemed to be the best alternative on failure of furnishing a garrison of our own troops, which; for many reasons would be infinitely the most eligible mode, if the season and your means would possibly admit."

I have at the same time endeavored to take the best preparatory steps in my power for supplying the garrisons on the western

*As Fort Rensselaer, of Canajoharie, was only a picketed dwelling, he no doubt had reference to Fort Plain, and thus unwittingly adopted Gen. Van Rensselaer's new name for the principal post In the neighborhood,

waters by the provision contract. I can only form my magazine at Fort Herkimer, on the German flats, which is 32 miles by land and almost 50 by water from the carrying place between the Mohawk river and Wood creek (owing to the many curves). The route by the former is impracticable in its present state for carriages, and the other extremely difficult for bateaux, as the river is much obstructed with fallen and floating trees, from the long disuse of the navigation.

That nothing, however, which depends upon me might be left undone, I have -directed 10 months provisions for 500 men to be laid up at Fort Herkimer, and have ordered Col. Willett, an active officer commanding the troops of the State (he evidently meant State troops in that locality), to repair the roads, remove the obstructions in the river, and, as far as can be effected by the labors of the soldiers, build houses for the reception of the provisions and stores at the carrying place (Fort Stanwix), in order that the whole may be in perfect readiness to move forward, so soon as the arrangement shall be made with Gen. Haldimand. I shall have such ordnance and stores forwarded to Albany, as in the present view of matters may be judged necessary for the western posts, and I will also write to the Quartermaster-General, by this conveyance, on the subject of bateaux and the other articles, which may be required from his department. However, as I before observed, without money to provide some boats, and to pay the expense of transportation, it will be next to impossible to get these things even to Niagara."-*Sparks*.

From Princeton, New Jersey, October 12, 1783, Washington wrote to the Chevalier Chastelleux, as follows: "I have lately made a tour through the Lakes George and Champlain as far as Crown Point. Thence returning to Schenectada, I proceeded up the Mohawk river to Fort Schuyler (formerly Fort Stanwix), and crossed over to Wood creek, which empties into the Oneida lake, and affords the water communication with Ontario. I then traversed the country to the eastern branch of the Susquehanna, and viewed the Lake Otsego, and the portage between that lake and the Mohawk river at Canajoharie. Prompted by these actual observations, I could not help taking a more expensive view of the vast inland navigation of these United States, from maps and the information of others, and could not but be struck with the immense extent and importance of it, and with the goodness of that Providence, which has dealt its favors to us with so profuse a hand. Would to God we may have wisdom enough to improve them. I shall not rest contented, till I have explored the western country, and traversed those lines or a great portion of them, which have given bounds to a new empire. But when it may, if it ever shall happen, I dare not say, as my first attention must be given to the deranged situation of my private concerns, which are not a little injured by almost nine years absence and total disregard of them, etc., etc."

The reader will observe by Washington's correspondence, that he made the northern trip by water to Crown Point, but from Schenectada to Fort Stanwix, or rather its site, on horseback. The tour of inspection as shadowed in his letters, is devoid of all incident, and whether or not he halted at Fort Plain on his way up is uncertain; but as he speaks last of going to Otsego Lake, it is presumed he made no halt at the river forts going up, nor is there any mention of his visiting Johnstown in his tour, but it is reasonable to conclude that he did.

He did not mention Fort Plain, but it is well known that he was there, giving it another name. Arriving in its vicinity, said the late Cornelius Mabee, who was thus informed by his mother, he tarried over night with Peter Wormuth, in Palatine, on the late Reuben Lipe farm, the former having had an only son killed, as elsewhere shown, near Cherry Valley. It was no doubt known to many that he had passed up the valley, who were on the *quivive* to see him on his return, and good tradition says that in the morning many people had assembled at Wormuth's to see the world's model man, and to satisfy their curiosity, he walked back and forth in front of the house, which fronted toward the river. This old stone dwelling in ruins, was totally demolished about the year 1863.

We have seen that Washington found Col. Willett in command at Fort Herkimer on his visit, at which time Col. Clyde was in command of Fort Plain. Just how many accompanied his Excellency through the Mohawk valley, is not satisfactorily known. His correspondence only names Gov. George Clinton.

Campbell, in his Annals, says he was accompanied by Gov. Clinton, Gen. Hand, and many other officers of the New York line. But his retinue was not a large one. The officers making the escort were no doubt attended by their aids and servants. Whether any other officer remained with Washington at Wormuth's over night is unknown. It is presumed, however, the house being small and the fort only a mile off, that his attendants all went thither, crossing at Walrath's Ferry, opposite the fort, some of whom returned in the morning to escort the Commander-in-chief over the river.

A pretty incident awaited his arrival on the eminence near the fort. Beside the road Rev. Mrs. Gros had paraded a bevy of small boys, her nephew Lawrence Gros (from whom this fact was derived) being of the number, to make their obeisance. At a signal they took off and swung their hats, huzzaed a welcome and made their best bow to Washington, when the illustrious guest gracefully lifted his chapeau, returned their respectful salutation with a cheerful, "Good morning, boys!"* Immediately after, he rode up to the fort where he received a military salute from the garrison.

I suppose Washington to have been welcomed within the large block-house, and on introducing the guest to its commandant, Gov. Clinton took occasion to say to him: "Gen. Washington, this is Col. Clyde, a true whig and a brave officer who has made great sacrifices for his country." The guest responded with warmth: "Then, sir, you should remember him in your appointments." From this hint Gov. Clinton afterwards appointed him sheriff of Montgomery county. The distinguished guest dined with Col. Clyde,+ after which,

*In 1880, I was assured by the venerable Jabez Tappen, then residing near Fort Plain, that when a boy he lived at Morristown, N. J. When Washington was on his way to New York, to be inaugurated as president, in April, 1789, his uncle Stephen Ogden, his mother's brother, stood beside the road with three sons, Charles, Ephraim and Jacob, and informant, and as Washington neared the little platoon powdered and ruffled, they doffed their hats and holding them against their left breast with their right hands, they made their best bow to the Illustrious traveler. The hero touched his beaver gracefully, and with a gesture of the hand he said, "Good morning, sirs." He was escorted from Morristown to Trenton by a body of cavalry. Ogden was a soldier under Washington at Monmouth, where he was terribly wounded, and where be was personally noticed by Washington, as he lay upon the ground, with a bullet through the hips.

+ Since the above was written, I have learned the following facts, In the history of Col. Samuel Clyde. He was born in Windham, Rockingham county, N. H., April 11, 1732: his mother's maiden name being Esther Rankin. He worked his father's farm, to the age of 20, when he went to Cape Breton and worked as a ship-carpenter, from whence he went to Halifax and labored on a dock for the English navy. In 1757, he went to New Hampshire and raised a company of bateau-men and rangers, of which he was appointed Captain, by Gen. James Aberoromby, said company being under the command of Lieut. Col. John Bradstreet. This commission was dated at Albany, May 25, 1758. He marched his company to Albany, and was soon after on his way to Lake George. He was in the battle of Ticonderoga, in which Gen. Howe was slain, and the British defeated. He was afterwards at the capture of Fort Frontenac and returning from the campaign to Schenectada, In 1761, he there married Catharina Wasson, a niece of Matthew

Thornton, a signer of the declaration of Independence. In 1762, he became a permanent settler of Cherry Valley. About the year 1770, Capt. Clyde erected a small church, for the Indians, at Oneida castle, which with graced with an English bell, at the first ringing of which the Indians manifested unbounded joy.

escorted by Maj. Thornton, they proceeded to Cherry Valley, where they became the guests, over night, of Col. Campbell, "who had returned not long before and erected a log house. Judge Campbell in his Annals, erroneously dates this visit in 1784 instead of 1783. Burnt out as the Campbell's had been, their accommodations were limited for so many guests, but they were all soldiers and had often been on short allowance of "bed and board," and could rough it if necessary. Besides, it is possible other families had returned to discover their hospitality for the night. They found themselves very agreeably entertained, however. Mrs. Campbell and her children had been prisoners to Canada.

In the morning Gov. Clinton, seeing several of her boys, told Mrs. Campbell "they would make good soldiers in time." She replied, "she hoped their services would never be thus needed."

"I hope so, too, madam," said Washington, "for I have seen enough of war." One of those boys, the late Judge James S. Campbell, was captured so young and kept so long among the Indians, that he could only speak their language when exchanged. After breakfast, the party were early in the saddle to visit the outlet of Otsego Lake, and see where Gen. James Clinton dammed the lake just above its outlet, to float his boats down the Susquehanna, to join in Sullivan's expedition. We saw several of the posts of that dam, still in the water, about the year 1845. The party returned the same evening to Fort Plain, via the portage road, opened by Clinton to Springfield from Canajoharie, and the next day, as believed,

*Said Judge Hammond, in *Stuart's Magazine:* In 1852, Mrs. Clyde, whom he had the pleasure of knowing, was a woman of uncommon talents both natural and acquired, and of great fortitude. She read much and kept up with the literature of the day. Her style in conversing was peculiarly elegant, and at the same time easy and unaffected. Her manner was dignified, graceful and attractive. Her conversation with young men during the Revolutionary war, tended greatly to raise their drooping spirits, and confirm their resolution to stand by their country to the last." Not a few noble women on the frontiers thus made their influence felt in the hour of need.

they dropped down the valley.-*Judge George Clyde*, and *Judge W. W. Campbell.*

At the beginning of national difficulties, a company of volunteers was raised in Cherry Valley and New Town Martin for home protection, of which Samuel Clyde was commissioned its Captain, by the 40 men he was to command, of which John Campbell, Jr., was chosen Lieutenant, and James Cannon, Ensign. Among the names of the volunteers voting for these officers, appears that of Samuel Campbell, afterwards Colonel. This commission was dated July 13, 1775. October 28, following the State Prov. Congress commissioned him as a Captain and Adjutant of the First Regiment of Tryon county militia. September 5, 1776, he was commissioned as Second-Major of the fourth regiment, commanded by Col. Cox. Here is an error in the number of the regiment, as Cox commanded the First from the promotion of Gen. Herkimer. June 25, 1778, Maj. Clyde was appointed Lieutenant-Colonel of the regiment, of which Samuel Campbell was then Colonel, the commission as such passing the secretary's office with the signature of Gov. George Clinton, March 17, 1781. He must have had borne evidence of his appointment long before. We have not seen his commission as Colonel of this regiment which he attained to.

That Clyde was the acting Colonel of this regiment long before the date of his commission as Lieutenant-Colonel, here is positive evidence. A company of Levies was being raised in Tryon county, and under date of May 3, 1780, Stephen Lush, upon consulting with Gen. Ten Broeck and Col. Van Schaick, wrote to the Colonels of the valley regiments, to write names in commissions inclosed, for a Captain and a Lieutenant of said company. This letter was thus superscribed:

"Public Service -George Clinton-Colonels Klock, Fisher, Clyde and Bellinger-any three or two of them-Tryon county." Those were the acting Colonels of the Tryon county militia at that date, as recognized in Albany. Col. Clyde seems to have been on duty every summer in the bounds of his regiment, until the close of the war.

On the organization of the State government in 1777, he was a member of the Legislature. March 8, 1785, he was commissioned as sheriff of Montgomery county, by George Clinton, March 8, 1785; the duties of which office he discharged with conscientious fidelity.-*Clyde Manuscripts*, and Hon. J. D. *Hammond's Sketch* published in 1852.

And I here mention with deep regret, that Isaac De Graff, his compatriot and friend, stated to me in 1844 (then at the age 87), while speaking of the virtues and goodness of Col. Clyde, that owing to his unbounded generosity he became involved, and was confined in the Otsego county jail for debt, where he soon after died. This fact is not mentioned as a stigma upon his character for it was not-as many a good man at that period was thus incarcerated for lenity and assistance rendered to others-but to show how the most deserving, were at times affected by that cruel law, which imprisoned a virtuous man for his own or someone's else debts.

After the destruction of Cherry Valley, Col. Campbell is said to have made his home at Niskayuna, and is not remembered as taking an active part in military affairs after that event in 1778. Whether or not he retained his commission as Colonel of the regiment while Clyde was discharging its duties, is unknown to the writer; but the late date of Clyde's commission as Lieutenant-Colonel, would seem to imply such a state of things. Certainly Gov. Clinton must have known who the acting Colonel of the regiment in question was, after 1778 to the close of the war.

No. 252
$13.59

City of New-York, ſs.

To Daniel Phœnix, Treasurer.

Pay Andrew Leary. Thirteen —

Dollars 59/100 —   for Cartage on account

of Streets —   Aug.ᵗ 10. 1807

By order of Common Council,

John Pintard.
Clerk.

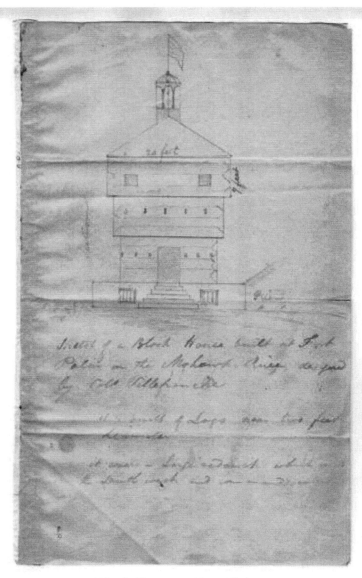

Block House at Fort Plain.

General Washington Arrives at Fort Rensselaer July 28, 1783

Miscellaneous Letters and Documents
Concerning Marinus Willett

Schenectady 6th Febry 1783

4 O Clock

My dear sir

Yours by Captain [Jellis A.] Fonda come save [sic, safe] to hand & have openied your meaning I am unhappy I have not seen you Goeing & Comeing from home yesterday my Business Called me to Alb[any]y when I called at your Brothers But you was Gone on I took it when I got home you had Gone above this place I Got home at Eight OClock—The moment I recd yours I whent [sic, went] for the Incampment ware my Regiment Lys [sic, lays] & Got Johnjost & Capt John Otaawightow a very prudent Savage & a man that Cane [sic, can] be dependd [sic, depended] on Ready for the Randesous [Sic, Rendezvous] you had orderd which is F Renselier who I now Send to you & Flatter my self will [???] they are both Trouble Some when in Liquor particular Jonjost who when drunck not by his Sincies [sic, senses] Varily one of the Conjiatures [sic, Coinjectures] Since you have past this City & the more & Since a number of Slays [sic, sleighs] with Armed men Past Likewise as the matter of the Troops marching from the north to the Westward Give a large field for Conjictur[e]s I must think tho no Great thinker my self of their was some thing in the wind.

Should that be the Cause no man shall be more happier in to learn the Success of the Expedition than your truely friend if its not consisted with the duty you owe your Country to tell me by a line before your Departure & Conveyed me by a save hand I am equally Contended shall pray your Save Return to one who is near & dear who is Mrs. Willott more friends I must Concluded [sic, Conclude] with my Best wishes for your Save Return fi you Got at all times my wishes will adtend[sic, attend] you ware Ever you Go I will all most Insure you Success shoul[d] you Got to the part of O:n if you Carry your Slays as far as West End of On dia [sic, Oneida] Leake [sic, lake] & no father-three days After that will do the Job & two back to the slays—

I am with the Greatest Sincirety

Yours & very humble Servt.

H. Glen

To Col M Willott

P.S. Since writing this letter Jonjost Got in the frowlking [sic, Frolicing] a [torn] sun sitt to Go for which I have optained [sic, Obtained] another one in his place whos[e]name is peter [torn] [?] the schame at home the Chief of the [?] are on the Hunt. H. Glen

To Colonel M. Willlott Commanding

The Troops west ward

By Capt John & Tryon County

Jonjost 2 Indians Fort Renselier

FROM: New York State Library. SC 16670, Box 1, Folder 17.

Lieutenant Albert Roose.

Staatsburgh 5th January 1783.

Sir,

On my arrival at this place I received a Letter from Colo. Willett, the following is an Extract.

I wish you to send me as soon as possible the names of all the Officers, & the number of men they have recruited for the two years service & Inform those officers that I shall be glad to see themselves & what men they may have at this place by the first day of February at Farthest—should any of the men have received promise of have leave of absence from the regiment for a longer time then to the first of February they may be assured that they shall have furlough to make up the time they may have been promised to be furlough to-- But I have received particular directions to have the whole of the men present for Inspection at that time. I must therefore request you to exert yourself in forwarding the whole of the men raised by Captain White &

Livingston for any of there Subaulterns to this place by the time aforesaid.

I have sent returns to the Colonel of the number of men recruited & the names of the Officers that recruited them Your own return I sent & the number of men I sent was fifteen (your full complement) ten you recruited & three I have got for you & two more you told me you had the promise of which makes your complement of fifteen.

I wish to see you at my house as soon as possible if not you will march your men to Fort Rensselear by the time appointed. I would not advise you to bring your men over for muster that can be done at Albany. I propose to be in Albany about the 20ᵗʰ of this Month.

Pray give my best respect to Uncle Garret V. Gelder, wishing to see him at my house with yourself.

I am Sir with sentiments of Esteem your very Humb'l Servant. J. Pearsee

Lt. Albert Roose

FROM: New York State Library, Document No. 16263.

Albany July 2d 1781.

Sir,

This moment I have received his Excellency's orders to put the regular Troops under my command in immediate motion for West point It is my request therefore that immediately on the receipt of this you collect all the Levies of your Regt when you think can be spared that are on the different Stations on the Mohawk River and relieve Col [Philip Van Courtlandt at Fort Herkimer. It will be necessary that you direct Capt [Philip] Canine to proceed to Schoharie—You will no doubt [be] in the necessity as Capt [Henry] DBois of Courtlandt's regt must move of]f] affording any Assistance in your power to compleat the Troops—the Fort on the proposed Plan: and assure the Inhabitants that a Considerable Body of Militia from the Eastward are directed to march to their Assistance, and that nothing but absolute Necessity would have induced the Genl [George Washington] to Order the Troops from the Frontier—Genl [John] Starks [I expect every is crossed out] will take the Command whose Arrival I wait—he will take his Quarters at Saratoga—I have Countermanded the Orders for Majr [John McKinstry to march, except that Company of Capt [Anthony] Whelps whom you had directed to join you.

I have no doubt but that you will endeavor to inspirit the Militia, and obtain every Assistance from them in your power— And a[s] there are a Considerable Quantity of Stores now at Fort Herkimer I would advise [that is crossed out], if you think [your is crossed out] whem unsafe with the Troops you will have with you, to send them down [??] deal them out with a Careful Hand.
Col Willet

End notes by the State Historian, Hugh Hastings in preparation for publishing. This is a proof copy, because of the big fire called the Capital Fire in 1911, the project was abandoned.

148 GANSEVOORT PAPERS (No. 18)
At the request of Gen. Stirling a Copy of Gen. Heath's congratulatory Order is Forwarded to Gansevoort.
Head Quarters Albany Novem. 13, 1781.
Sir: Enclosed is a Copy of Major General Heath's Orders which I send you by request of M. Gen'l Lord Stirling and am, Sir, Your most Ob. Servant.
Thos. Fred'k Jackson, (1) Aide De camp.
Gen. Gansevoort.

1. Thomas Frederick Jackson was aide to Gen. Heath in the skirmish at Montressor's Island In 1776; at the battle of Stillwater in 1777; at the battle of Monmouth in 1778; and in Springfield, N.J. in 1780.

Major General William Heath's Congratulatory Proclamation on Col. Willett's Victory.

Head Quarters Continental Village, Novem. 9, 1781.

The General has the pleasure of acquainting this Army that the Enemy has been completely disappointed in their designs on the Northern Frontiers of this State in consequence of the measures adopted to receive them in the Vicinity of the Lakes, in which the General is much indebted to Major General Lord Stirling, Brigadier General Stark & the other Officers and Soldiers, both of the Regular troops & Militia who with great Zeal and alertness pressed to meet the Enemy—that part of their Force which was coming by way of the Lakes have not dared to land on this side of them.

Major Ross who had advanced form the Westward as far as Johnstown with a body of between Six & Seven Hundred Regular Troops, rangers, Yaugers, & Indians was met by Colonel Willett defeated and pursued into the Wilderness, where many of them probably must perish—the number of the "Enemy killed is not known—Major Butler who has frequently distressed the Frontiers is among the Slain. A number of prisoners chiefly British have bene taken and sent in.

The General presents his thanks to Colonel Willett whose address, Gallantry and preserving Activity exhibited on this occasion do him the highest Honor, and while the Conduct of the Officers and Soldiers in General who were with Coll. Willett deserve high commendation the General expresses a particular approbation of the behavior of Major Rowley & of the brave Levies & Militia under his immediate Command who at a critical Moment not only did Honor to themselves, but rendered a most essential service to their Country.

Transcript—from Gen'l Orders.

Thos. Fred'k Jackson,
Aide DeCamp.

Col. Abm. Wemple to Gansevoort—Ammunition Requested.

Schenectady, November 9th 1781.

Dear General: The inclosed is a letter just now received from Col. Pieter Vroman from Schoharie. I am. Sir, your Obt. Humble Servt.

P.S. please let me know if I can send tomorrow for the Ammunition that Lord Sterling ordered for me.

Peter Gansevoort, Esqr.

AND: *Fourteen Miles Above Schenectady—An appeal for Ammunition.*

Schenectady Octr. 25th 1781.

Sir: Just now an other Express is Arrived who brings the Disagreeable news that the Enemy are in great force and were this afternoon at 3 OClock engaged at fort Hunter. A body of 350 Red Coats have been seen marching along the Road about 14 miles above this place.

We have reasons to believe that the Enemy are Strong. We Expect to be Attacked this night. If possible send us some reinforcement soon.

N.B. the enclosed is just Come to hand. For God sake send some ammunition. A.W.

Peter Gansevoord Esqr.

Brigadr. Gen'l

Per Express Albany.

James Winney to Henry Glen—Willett's Fight at Johnstown.

Sir: The Enemy are in Johnstown (1). The last Accounts we have from there was that Colonel Willett (2) had lost his field Piece and that he had Retreated into the fort at that Place. I was on my way to join him but Received the above Intelligence on my way which made me retreat to this Place. I have met a Good many of this County Militia here, several of whom will go with me to Johnstown this Night. I am Sir Your Hum.Servt. Jas.Winney.

Veders Mills 25th (1781) Octbr. 8 O Clock P.M.

There has been a Severe Ingagement.

Public Service.

Express: Henry Glen. Esquire A.D.Q. M. Schenectady.

1. Intelligence having been received that Major John Ross, with from 500 to 700 British troops, Loyalists and Indians, was coming down the Mohawk, Colonel Willett went up to meet him, leading his regiment of New York levies, some New York militia and a small body of Massachusetts militia under Major Aaron Rowley. Ross drew off in the direction of Johnstown, and a little north of this place the two forces came in contact. Rowley had been detached to make a circuitous movement and fall upon the rear of the Royalists with so much spirit that they were thrown into confusion, whereupon the New York levies rallied and pressed the attack with irresistible energy. Long after Ross' command was put to flight, the Americans pursued their scattered forces. Fifty-two prisoners were brought in; and of the enemy's fallen the patriot commander gave the following account: "Unless the swamps and rivers in which they fell were to report the killed, it was impossible to make a return of them." Among the slain was Walter N. Butler, the detested partisan leader, who fell at the hands of the Oneidas. The American losses were 13 killed, 23 wounded, 5 missing. State Historian.

2. See Clinton Papers, Vol VII, p. 443-444; 447-448.

I do hereby certify that on pursuit of the enemy in the County of Montgomery the latter end of October in the year 1781. In order to stimulate a party of the Oneida Indians then with me. I promised in case of exerting themselves to overtake the enemy who were put to flight. That they should each of them have a blanket—That in consequence of this promise they began a vigorous pursuit and in a short time overtook and killed a number of the enemy—That at my return it was not in my power to comply with the promise I had made in behalf of the public. Nor have I since been able to have that engagement complied with—New York January 26th 1792.

M Willett

Note there were sixty Indians in the party

M Willett

Original Letter in The Johnstown Historical Society.

Some interesting documents from Witter Johnston's Pension Papers. The following deals with getting things done to close down the service of the men who participated.

Albany 4th July 1782
Colonel Willetts Orders

His Excellency the Governor having directed the Companies of such officers as have furnish'd thare Quotas of men for the Two and three years Service be completed out of the Levies and that the whole off the two years men and Levies Raisd in this Quota be incorporated and fraimd [sic, formed] into one Regiment to Be completed Agreeable to the Continental Astablishment. [Establishment]

And it Apearing [appearing] that three of the Captains who whare [were] to Raise men for two years on Bounty of unappropriated Lands have furnished thare Quotas of men and in as much as the whole of two years men and Levies is not more than sufficient to compliet [complete] one Regiment to Consist of nine companies; three companies of Levies must of corse [coursc] become Anilated [Annihilated]—The men of these companies are then Aneset [sic, annexed] to such Companies as have not thare Quotas and the Officers become Deranged—the following officers are to form the Corps for this Regiment of Levies and men raised for two and three years incorporated together. [names are as they appear and not always capitalized.]

Captains	Subalterns	Subalterns
Abraham Livingston	Victor Putman	Josiah Richardson
Jonathan Pearsee	John Thornton	Mathew Trotter
Abner French	Yellis Funda	Jessey hubble
Job Wright	Peter Van Bergen	Rial Bingham
Guy Young	Duncan Cambell	Oliver Newell
	Abraham Ten Eyck	John Shafer
Joseph Harrison	Timothy hutton	John Watson

Peter B. Tears	Peter Loop	Jon'n hilton
		Witter Johston
James Cannon	Pliny Moor	Lawrence Trimper
Simeon Newel	Thomas Skinner	John Hums'd
	Storm Becker	

Capt henrys Compiny is to be Aneset to the Companies of Capt Pearsee French Young Tierce & Newel Capt Grays to Captain Harrison & Cannon and Capt Welps to Capt Livingstons & Wright.

The Officers Commanding Compinies are Emediately on new fuarming [forming] of the Compinies to send Returns on the strenth [sic, strength] of thare Compinies to the Adjt at Skenactday [Schenectady] together with the names of the men they Receivd from the Compinies that become Annihalted [annihilated] at wich Place the Adjitant must attend to Receive them and Ajest them into a Regimental Return and Major Fink will will [sic] Attend the Quarters of Each Company to Inspect and Muster them for the Months of April May & June.

For the time to come Very Particular care is to be taken by officers commanding Compinies to have there Monthly Returns filled up on the Last Day of Every Month and forwarded to the Quarters of the Adjitant at Schanactidy the Names of any that have Died Deserted killed or taken Prisoners must be inserted on the Back of the Return.

These Returns must be Regudierly forwarded to the Quarters of the Adjtiant at Skenactidy the beginning of Every month no Excuse for Negligence of this Business can be Admitted.

By order of Colonel Willett
Jellis Funda, Adjt.

Fort Rancelor for Jany 7, 1783
Sir

You will March All the Men Under your command to this post with all posebel spead together with thare Baggage &c.
I am Sir Yours
E. Bunschoten
Leiut Johnson

John Davine has permission to stay at Johnstown until further orders. You will Draw provisions for him with the men under your command. M. Willett

Fort Rensselear
20th Jany 1783
Lieutenant Witter Johnson

Fort Renselear 15th January 1783.
This will be handed to you by Abra'm Van Horn Esqr who has promised me to explain to you a desire I have of getting you to Iraffic to me hides we have at this place for Leather The kind of leather and every thing else necessary for you to know respecting this business I have mentioned very particularly to Mr. Vank [???] you therefore to conform to what he may direct in this business without the least loss of time.

Capt Cannon tells me there are some spare shoes belonging to the publick at Johnstown. You will inquire very particulary how man pair there are and what condition they are in and make me acquainted with it.
I am Sir with much
Esteem your Very
Humble Servt
M. Willett

Fort Rensselaer 22d Dec'r 82.
Sir

You will repair with the men you have in charge to Johnstown where you are to take post untill further orders—you are to keep out small scouts towards and beyond the Secondaoga or any other pass through which you may have reasin to apprehend any parties to or from the enemy may make their routs--

As the destrict in which you are to be posted is Inhabited by a number of Dissafected persons you are watchfully to observe their Conduct—And endeavor to find out any Intercouse they may have with the enemy—

Captain Cannon will leave a Carefull serjeant and Corporal with three good men from his Company with you to reinforce your Command.

On your Arrival at Johnstown you will Communicate my Orders to Captain Cannon to march the whole of his company now at Johnstown (Except those I have directed to be left with you) to this place. Together with the Detachment of Artillery And field piece which are posted there And to have all the Ammunition and other stores belonging to the Publick conveyed from Johnstown to this place.

I am Sir your
Very humble Servt
M. Willett Colonel Commandant.

Lieutenant Johnson
Fort Herkimer 16th 1782
Instructions for Lieut Johnston of New York State Levies you will take under your Command two Privets and proceed from this Post to Admesters [?] Place and make all the discovery you can of the [torn] if you should Discover any large Party you will give me the Earlest Information.

Abner French Capt. Commandt
Lieutenant Whit'r Jhonston [Johnston]

Vaders Mills 11th August 1782

Youll meet me at this Post to Morrow Morning 6 OClock in Order to proceed to your Muster Rolls. If your men are here at 1 o clock in the afternoon will be time enough as I expect to have one Roll Compleat & Muster them at that time.

Order all the men that can march to be here
Lieut Johnson
I am Sir Yours in haste Andrew Finck Maj'r

Sir You will immediately after the Receipt hereof send one Philip Philips a soldier under your charge to Kitmans Blockhouse.

By order of Major Bonschoten. Jellis A. Fonday, Ajg
Lieut Johnson

Vaders Mills July 18, 1782
Sir

You will immedaitley send one Furguson and Chapman down with the Bearer to Schenectady as they belong to Capt Cannon man.

I am yours
Jelles A. Fonda, Adj
Lieut. Johnson

Johnstown 14th June 1782
Dr Sir

You will march the men under your command to Vader Mills Tomorrow where you will Recve farder Instructions.

I am Sir your hbl Servt
E. Bunschoten
Lieut Johnson

Fort Schuyler November 3d 1783
Dr Sir,

I send by John Casler your Mare, and the papers of the Company agreeable to your request I keep your Knife & two forks till I come down myself I send you your small bundle of blue cloth your blankett was taken out of your Tent a day or two after you went away & Culver & Stillman never could give me any account of it. If you have any opportunity of sending home pray inform my friends that I am well my Compliments to all Inquring friends.

To Lieut Johnston

I remain

Dr. Sir

Your humble Servt

John Thornton

PS In your muster Rolls be particular in mentioned the time of the exchanges. I send you a Letter I received from Capt Tearse to assist you in making your Muster Rolls.

Fort Renselaer August 27th 1783

Dr Sir

I take this opportunity to inform you that you will be pleased to make out Two Muster Rolls as a desertion took place after I had maid mine out, not having time to Recopy the Sam as you may observe in this Roll I now send you the Casualties is herein expressed Excepting those men that will be on Command at fort Renselaer with me what I know not certainly by name at present but those that are absent you may put them under my Command at this post unless you receive further intelligence Endeavour to get your Number of Tents according to your no. of Men & furnish them in every respect with what is due to them as some Tents are better than others try to get the best.

The Liquor Bills you will receive & take care of being unwell, and detain'd here for further orders.

I am Dr Sir Your Obedient Sent. Jn Thornton

To Lieut Johnston

Fort Ranselaer 24th May 1783.
Sir

You'll proceed with the party under your Com'd and convey the Publick Boats at the Ferry (leaving one for the use of the Garrison) and all the other Publick Boats that you may find in the river between this place) & Schonectady and Deliver them to Henry Glen Esqr at that place, youll from thence proceed to the hellenburgh and endeavour to Apprehend A Certain Peter Tice, Corpl ham, a certain [Fash] supposed to be at Albany Bush & Joseph Clement at Tripes hill and Convey them to this place, if you should meet with any Deserters from the Regt you will cause them to be sent to the Regt with all possible Dispatch. I wish you success and

I am Sir your humble servant
To Lieut Johnson Andrew Finck Maj Comdt.

Sir

You are hereby directed to enter upon the [muster? Torn] of Recruiting Soldier for the two Regiments directed to [blotted & torn] for the defence of this State, agreeable to two Acts of the Leislature passed the 20th March 1781, and 23d March 1782. You are to offer an incouragement to Volunteers a right to five hundred Acres of unappropriated Lands, which Land they will be Intitled to receive at the Expiration of their times of Service without fee, reward, or Quit Rent reserved agreeable to the before recited Act of 20th March 1781—And as a further Incouragement of recruits to Enter into this Service, the public engages to Arm, Accouter, Subsist, and pay them in the same manner with the Continental Troops in the Service of the United States—But they are not to Serve out of the State without the consent of the Governor, or the person Administrating the Government of the State for the time being. You are authorised to inlist men for this Service out of the present Levies upon Condition of there [sic their] engaging to Serve two years from the first day of January next unless sooner discharged—Should any person willing to inlist for the Term above mentioned prefer money to the Lands Several Gentlemen who are desirous to to [sic] Encourage the Inlistment have engaged to pay to each Recruit Sixteen Dollars as soon as they are mustered, and will take the gratuity in Land offer'd by the State for the Money.

And for your own trouble and expence you may be at in this business you shall receive two Dollars for each recruit you may Engage on the Cash bounty.

M Willett Colo
Commandant
Lieut'nt Johnston

The following is a reprint of a book which is out of copyright, and is now public domain. It is worth the read and will give details of the service rendered by Lt-Col. Marinus Willett.

COL. MARINUS WILLETT.
The Hero of Mohawk Valley
An Address before The Oneida Historical Society.
By Daniel E. Wager.
Utica, N.Y. Printed for The Society. By the Utica Herald
Publication Company 1891.

Among the objects and purposes for which the Oneida Historical Society is organized, are the collection and preservation of materials relative to that part of New York formerly known as Tryon County. Within the scope of this organization is the gathering of scant and scattered materials, and weaving them into a narrative relative to the lives of those who have and been prominent foremost in the important and critical period of the existence of the county, and by their valor, patriotism and masterly activity made the valley of the Mohawk historic ground, and given to it a national importance in the history of the country. Of all the persons who have contributed to this grand result, I think I am safe in saying no one stands out more conspicuously than Col. Marinus Willett. It may be considered a fortunate conclusion that the gathering of materials for a sketch of his life should be no longer postponed, for it is evident that each year's delay lessens the chances and increases the difficulties of obtaining information not already recorded in the well-known histories of the times especially facts which can now be found only in unpublished manuscripts, or in the memory of living witnesses.

In my correspondence and inquiries for facts I luckily ascertained, what is probably known to but a comparatively few, that two sons of Col. Willett are yet alive, the one eighty-six and the other nearly eighty-eight years of age, with bright minds and unclouded intellects, who were able to impart much valuable information concerning their father, which but for their retentive memories and timely aid might have soon passed into hopeless oblivion.

Aside from the "narrative" of Col. Willett, written or dictated mainly, if not entirely by himself after he had attained his seventieth birthday, and published in 1831, the next year after his death, by the elder of the two sons aforementioned, there is no authentic sketch of his life extant. That "narrative" makes no mention of his civil career, which was quite a prominent one in New York, after the close of the revolutionary war, but has reference mainly to some of the more important military events with which he was connected; and even as to those, with the becoming modesty of a true soldier, but a brief narration is given.

But a few copies of that "narrative" are in existence, and those very difficult to be obtained. The details are too scant and meager to satisfy the longings of those who wish to know more of Col. Willett's life and character specially those of Tryon County, wherein he achieved his greatest victories, and won his grandest triumphs. So, too, the histories of the stirring times in which Col. Willett lived have not the space to do more than to mention incidentally, or briefly narrate the more prominent events of the stormy period of his life. Hence, it has been no easy matter, though to me a very pleasurable occupation, to glean from the various and widely separated fields of his active labors materials for a paper that will be full and accurate, and do justice to his merits and memory, and worthy of preservation in the archives of this society.

Thomas Willett, the first one of that family name who crossed the Atlantic to make his home in this western world, was born in England, where his father and grandfather had been ministers of the gospel. He came in the good ship Lion in 1632, when he was but twenty-two years of age, and settled in the

Plymouth colony, not far from the State line of Rhode Island. The records in that colony frequently mention his name, and furnish evidence that he became a person of wealth and prominence. In his young manhood he was a surveyor of highways, captain of a military company, and held other similar positions. He engaged in mercantile pursuits; was interested in sea-going vessels; owned large tracts of land, one of which was formed into a township by the name of "Swansea". In 1650, while a merchant of Plymouth, he was appointed by Peter Stuyvesant, then the Dutch colonial executive of New York, one of the boundary commissioners, to settle the disputed line between the English and Dutch. That line was adjusted, and has passed into history as the "Hartford boundary treaty of 1650".

After the English came into power in New York, Capt. Willett was appointed one of the councilors of that colony, and held that office from 1665 to 1673. In 1667 he was appointed by the English governor, Richard Nichols, the first English mayor of New York, from which it would appear he had, in the meantime, become a resident of the metropolis. When the Dutch, in 1673, regained ascendency in New York, the property of Thomas Willett was confiscated; he died the next year, at the age of sixty-four years, and his remains were buried at East Providence in Rhode Island. At page 59 of Lossing's History of the Empire State, a *fac simile* of Thomas Willett s signature can be found. He was the great grandfather of Col. Marinus Willett, whose name and fame are so closely and dearly associated with the history of Tryon County, during the stormy period of the revolutionary struggle.

Edward Willett (the father of Col. Willett,) was a Quaker and a farmer of moderate means, near Jamaica, on Long Island; at that homestead Marinus was born on July 31, 1740, (old style.) was the second son and child in a family of thirteen children, the same number that was born unto his great grandfather aforementioned. That father died in 1794, at the age of ninety-four years, and, although he belonged to a denomination that was on principle, opposed to war, yet he was destined to see two of his sons, before they were eighteen, enter the military service of their country, and the one to become a prominent leader; the other to be a lieutenant on an English privateer, and the vessel on which he was engaged swept away in a hurricane in the French war of 1758, and all on board lost at sea. Marinus, until he was nearly eighteen years of age, pursued the quiet and peaceful pursuits of a farm life at his father s homestead. About that period of his life, he was moved by a spirit of self-reliance to leave the paternal roof and provide for himself. With a resolute will and a determined spirit, and with only twenty shillings in his pocket, he crossed over to New York to seek in that great city employment, and, it possible, make his fortune.

It was about the time of the French war of 1758, when the colonists were greatly excited by reason of raising of troops, and the activity of the contending forces. In the early spring of that year, three English expedition^ were being fitted out, with a view to attack the French at different points, and drive them out of this country. One of those expeditions, and in which New York took the greatest interest, was under the command of General Abercrombie, and to be led by him from Albany to lakes George and Champlain to attack Fort Ticonderoga, then garrisoned by 4,000 troops under Montcalm a field marshal of France. Here were to be raised in the vicinity New York three battalions of 900 men each, to be under the command of Col. Oliver DeLancey, a brother of the acting governor of New York.

It required no great effort to raise the requisite number of troops, for the whole country was in commotion, and the people running over with enthusiasm. Young Willett caught the prevailing spirit of the times and, following his own ambition and the example of others, he enlisted in the army and raised a company of soldiers on Long Island among his neighbors and acquaintances. Through the influence of friends, he was appointed second lieutenant of his company, and, although not then eighteen years old, he was as full of patriotism and spirit as those of maturer years. In his "narrative" is the following description of the uniform he wore on receiving his commission as lieutenant, viz.: "Green coat trimmed with silver twist; white under clothes and black gaiters, a cocked hat with large black cockade of silk ribbon, with silver button and loop". The three battalions were raised, and the first week in May the troops left New York in sloops, ascended the Hudson to Albany, thence marched overland to Schenectady, and for two weeks were employed in patrolling the Mohawk to watch the settlements and prevent an attack from the French, if one should be made in that quarter.

Orders then came to march to Lake George, where they arrived the fore part of June, and found that active preparations were there going forward to cross the lake. The last of the month Gen. Abercrombie arrived, but the soul of the expedition and the idol of the army was young Lord Howe, then thirty-four years of age; young Willett has left on record his high appreciation of the ability and soldierly qualities of that gallant officer. Soon after daybreak on Sunday, July 5th, the whole army, 16,000 strong, embarked in 1,000 boats, to cross Lake George, from its southern extremity, to its northerly shore. The day was bright and clear, the soldiers were clad in their scarlet coats, and as this armament floated upon the glassy surface of this inland sea, accompanied by martial music, while ensigns and banners floated in the breeze and glittered in the sunbeams, it looked more like a holiday occasion than an army going to battle.

At dawn the next morning, the troops landed at the north end of the lake, some four or five miles from Fort Ticonderoga, and while reaching the shore, had a slight skirmish with the occupants of a French outpost at that point, in which a couple of Frenchmen were killed. A few of the Stockbridge tribe of Indians accompanied this expedition, and as soon as they saw the two dead soldiers they rushed forward and secured their scalps. This was young Willett s first experience in witnessing the scalping process, but those scenes became familiar to him later in life. The country between Lake George and Fort Ticonderoga was covered by a dense forest and tangled morasses; the troops formed in good order, and commenced marching by columns through the woods. Lord Howe led the advance guard, near whom was the regiment in which young Willett marched, moving forward to exposed points of danger and expecting every moment to fall into an ambush or to be met by a strong French force. The eve of battle is always one of breathless anxiety, especially to those who have never been in an engagement or witnessed one. This was Willett's first experience, and he has left an account of his feelings on this occasion; he states that he did not at this time, nor ever subsequently in his life, experience the slightest degree of fear, but on the contrary he was quite elated, and his spirits highly exhilarated as the crisis approached.

The troops had not proceeded two miles before an ambush was discovered near where young Willett was marching. A sharp engagement ensued and Lord Howe was soon to the front rallying and cheering his men, when he was struck by a bullet and instantly killed. The French were dispersed, but the sudden death of Howe threw his troops into confusion and disorder. There then seemed to be no leader or anyone to issue orders. The troops wandered about following incompetent guides, crossing each other's track, and firing at their own friends, mistaking them, for the foe. While thus moving Willett and his companions accidentally fell in with Gen. Abercrombie, who stood under a huge tree, with a large cloak wrapped about him, while two regiments of regular troops were drawn up around his person to guard and protect him from harm. He issued no orders and the troops continued to wander the rest of the day, lost and bewildered in the woods. As night overtook them, they halted and rested until morning; on awaking it was found that most of the men had encamped near the spot where they had landed from the boats the morning before.

It was afternoon before the army was again in motion for Fort Ticonderoga, and when three miles from the fort, they halted and passed another night in the woods. The next day, which was the 8th of July, the army again started on its march for the fort, and about noon was re-enforced by six hundred Indians under the command of Sir William Johnson. But the want of a leader and competent guides had not been supplied. The same confusion, disorder and bewilderment prevailed, and before the troops were aware of it, or knew the danger they were in, they became entangled in a network of fallen trees, and found they were directly under the enemy s breastworks, and exposed to a murderous fire. For four or five hours the battle raged, to the great disadvantage of the British troops, and it was not until sunset the firing ceased, and the latter retired to spend another night in the forest, expecting to renew the attack the next day, before daylight.

The next morning Lieut. Willett was awakened from a sound sleep and told that the army was rapidly making its way to their boats, with a view to recross the lake. About eight that morning the troops re-embarked, and, although there was no enemy near, great confusion and disorder prevailed, and this expedition, which, three days before, came with such pomp and splendor, returned in disgrace, leaving behind it, killed and wounded, some two thousand of its numbers. No doubt Gen. Abererombie felt much safer when he had put thirty-eight miles of Lake George between himself and Montcalm.

In that expedition were two other persons prominent in the history of New York, and who have been more or less connected with affairs in Tryon county. The one was Gen. Philip Schuyler, whose name was given to Fort Stanwix during a portion of the revolutionary war; the other, Gen. John Bradstreet, a prominent officer in the colonial service, and who was, for years, part owner of Cosby's manor, which includes the site of Utica, and whose widow, by another marriage, was grandmother to that Martha Bradstreet who made her name famous, not only by reason of her legal and other abilities, but by the long, tedious and expensive litigation which, over half a century ago, she inflicted upon Uticans and others, regarding their land titles. Gen. Bradstreet was but a major in that expedition, yet he burned with indignation because of its shameful failure.

At a council of war held at the head of the lake the very evening the troops returned from Ticonderoga, he urged the adoption of measures that would tend to wipe out or relieve the disgraceful blunder. He suggested an expedition against Fort Frontenac (now Kingston,) and offered to lead it. Some looked upon such an undertaking as wild and chimerical, and its successful execution improbable, for it was considered a strong fortress for those times, well supplied with men, cannon and ammunition; but Bradstreet urged his offer with so much earnestness that Gen. Abererombie at last reluctantly consented to commission him to go and take with him three thousand troops.

Among the number was young Willett and the regiment to which he belonged. The destination was kept secret from all but the leading officers. They started the next day and were moved with greatest rapidity to Albany, thence to the Mohawk, and they "fairly flew", as it is said, up the river in boats, to the "Oneida carrying place," now the site of Rome. And here let me add, by way of parenthesis, that besides Schuyler and Willett, who accompanied Gen. Bradstreet to Fort Frontenac, were many others who subsequently became noted in the history of this country. Among them Nathaniel Woodhull, then a major, subsequently a general in the revolutionary army, and the first president of the provincial congress; Horatio Gates, then a captain and in the revolutionary war a brigadier general, and who captured Burgoyne and his army; Col. Charles Clinton, then stationed at Fort Herkimer, and near seventy years of age; also his two sons, James Clinton, then a captain and twenty-two years old, afterward a general, and his brother George, then nineteen years old, and afterwards for twenty-five years governor of New York; the great war governor of the infant State.

Although Gen. Bradstreet moved his men up the valley with great celerity, yet it took two weeks' time for the men to pole the boats up the river to the "carrying place". On reaching this portage, Gen. John Stanwix was found with six thousand troops, having been previously ordered there to erect a formidable fort in the place of Forts William, Craven, and Bull, destroyed two years before. The first two named forts had stood upon the banks of the Mohawk, below the bend of that river, a little further downstream than the present railroad bridge. Fort Bull was upon the lower landing of Wood Creek, some two or three miles to the westward of Forts Craven and William.

Across this portage Bradstreet transported his men, boats and munitions of war and stores. A dam was constructed across Wood Creek, at the upper landing near the late United States arsenal, to raise the water of that stream, to aid in floating the loaded boats to Oneida Lake. Two weeks' time was occupied in making these preparations, and in removing the fallen trees and other obstructions from the creek. These movements indicated to the troops the direction of the expedition. The troops started August 14 and in six days Oswego was reached; after resting there for a few hours to repair the boats, inspect the arms and accoutrements, the troops were again on their way passing over the lake, but keeping near shore. On the third day after leaving Oswego, the troops landed on the evening of the 25th, about two miles from the fort, and the next day commenced active preparations to take it by storm. The fort was a square one, fifteen feet high, built of stone and nearly three-fourths of a mile in circumference, and well protected by cannon; the garrison had no intimation of the approach of an enemy, until the British troops appeared before the fortress. Breastworks were erected to protect the assailants, and Willett was much of the time in exposed points of danger, and one entire night he and his men were under a constant tire of grape shot and musketry.

The siege was continued for three days, and on the 29th of August the garrison surrendered; the capture included sixty cannon, sixteen mortars, a vast amount of small arms, a large quantity of powder and balls of all sorts, nine vessels and about one hundred men. The magazine was blown up, the buildings destroyed, and the whole fortress reduced to a heap of rubbish. The captured vessels were used to transport the stores to Oswego, and there burned to the water s edge.

The capture of this fort was considered at the time, as one of the greatest blows inflicted upon the French in America, considering the consequences, as that fort was the storehouse from which other forts to the south were supplied. It reflected great credit upon Bradstreet and his men, although it involved incessant toil, great fatigue and hardship, and a great sacrifice of human life. When Oswego Falls (now Fulton) was reached by the troops on their return from Oswego, it took the men three days to drag the boats and stores over that portage of a mile, and so excessive was the labor, and so great the fatigue and exposure of the men in the whole expedition that near one hundred deaths occurred at that point, and when Fort Bull was reached half of the men were unfit for duty. It required four days to transport the boats and stores from Wood Creek across the portage at Rome, to the Mohawk, and by that time the men were completely exhausted. Smith's Colonial History of New York says that five hundred men died and were buried at this "carrying place". The cause of these deaths and sickness, is attributed to the stagnant water of Wood Creek, the exposure and fatigue of the men, and the haste in cooking the food.

The expedition on its return, reached Fort Stanwix September 10, and that very night young Willett was taken ill and confined to his tent until November by a dangerous illness. As before stated, that was the season Fort Stanwix was constructed. The work was commenced August 23 and completed November 15, 1758. It was a square work, bounded by what are now Dominick, Spring, and Liberty streets, and was about 20 rods westerly from the Mohawk. It was surrounded by a deep, wide ditch, with long pickets in the center, sharpened at the top, and a row of horizontal ones projected from the embankment. It was among the most formidable structures of the times and cost the British government over $266,000.

After Lieutenant Willett partially recovered his health and strength he was put in a boat and taken down the river to Schenectady; thence overland to Albany where he remained until December 1. The ice in the meantime having left the Hudson, he went down that river in a boat and reached New York the 7th of December, just seven months to a day from the time he had left that city in such good health and high spirits to join Abercrombie s expedition.

His feeble health and the wishes of his friends prevented his taking any further part in the war. In fact, that war was near its close, for the success of the British arms the next year, the taking of Quebec in September, witnessed the culminating genius and crowning glory of Wolfe, and the valor and heroic death of Montcalm, and practically put an end to French domination on this continent.

I have not learned the occupation of Col. Willett between the close of the French war and the commencement of the revolution. The eldest son writes me, that he never heard it mentioned, but that when he was a lad, a piece of household furniture was pointed out in the dwelling as the workmanship of his father, which leads to the inference that Col. Willett might have been a cabinetmaker in his early manhood; but nothing further has been ascertained. Certain it is, however, that in whatever vocations he engaged, he was always abreast of the times and kept himself well informed as to politics and the current events of the day, and was ever found arrayed on the side of freedom and the rights of man.

In 1765 occurred the popular and universal outbreak in the colonies, caused by the threatened enforcement of the odious stamp act; but for the timely repeal of that law, the revolutionary conflict in the colonies, might have been precipitated ten years sooner than it was. In October, 1765, while a colonial congress of delegates was in session in New York City, a vessel arrived in port, bringing the obnoxious stamps. The law was to go into effect November 1. The stamps were unloaded from the vessel and hurriedly conveyed to and lodged in the fort in that city, then garrisoned by British troops.

A body of men called "The Sons of Liberty" were organized and among the prominent leaders, was young Marinus Willett, then twenty-five years old. When it was known the stamps had arrived and lodged in the fort, the whole city was in commotion; a large and tumultuous assemblage convened in the present city hall park, a gallows was erected and on it was hung an effigy of Gov. Colden. Another effigy of the governor was borne by an excited and exasperated crowd through the streets to the gate of the fort where soldiers were drawn up on the ramparts, but dare not fire. The stamps were demanded of the governor who refused to give them up, whereupon his carriage was seized, his effigy set upon it, the crowd marched to the battery, spiked the cannon and there burned carriage and effigy to ashes. The house of Major James, the commander of the royal artillery was attacked and gutted and the contents destroyed by fire and the colors of the regiment carried off by the populace.

The feeling was so intense and the excitement so great, the collector appointed to sell the stamps was afraid to act and resigned and no one dare use them. The people were appeased by assurances that the stamps should not be used, and in four months that law was repealed, never having been executed in any of the colonies. It was in times like these that young Willett took his first lessons in patriotism and learned to vindicate the rights of the people and prepared himself as an important factor in the revolutionary struggle which achieved American independence.

On Sunday, April 23, 1775, rumors spread through the city of New York that there had been a conflict between the people and the troops the Wednesday before at Lexington and Concord. The gale that carried that news over the land was but the slightest breeze of the approaching spirit of the storm. The feeling which incited brave old Gen. Putnam to unhitch his team, in the field where he was at work, leave the plow in the furrow, mount his horse and tear along the highway for one hundred miles to be leaguered Boston was the same which then spread itself into every hamlet throughout this broad land. The people of New York City, as if moved by one impulse, proceeded to the arsenal, forced open the door, took possession of six hundred muskets with bayonets and cartridge boxes and balls, and distributed these arms among the most active of the citizens; they formed themselves into a committee of safety and assumed the control of the city government. They took possession of the custom house and of all the public stores, cut loose two transports at the wharf, emptied the Vessels laden with provisions for Boston of their contents, seized the powder house, attempted to take possession of the magazine, published a declaration that no vessel should leave the fort for Boston; formed themselves into military companies and paraded the streets, but apparently with no definite object in view.

In the midst of this general commotion orders came from the British commander for the troops to proceed to Boston. The execution of this order could easily have been prevented, but for the timidity of some who were afraid to provoke a collision. The citizens held a meeting and agreed to allow the soldiers to depart with their own arms and accoutrements, but nothing else. One fine morning news spread like wildfire that the troops were embarking and were carrying off cartloads of chests of arms. Young Willett, who was one of the most active of the patriots, started out in one direction to notify his friends what was going on; while crossing Broad street he noticed the troops with five cart loads of arms coming down that street; without waiting for aid or advice he proceeded up the street, met the carts, took the foremost horse by the head. This brought things to a halt, and the major in command came forward to learn the cause; soon a crowd collected, and some of the committee opposed, and some approved the course of young Willett. Being encouraged and advised by his friends he mounted a cart, made a brief, stirring speech which was loudly cheered. He then turned the head of the forward horse into another street, those behind followed, and all of the carts were driven to a vacant lot and a ball alley on John Street, and thus the arms were prevented from leaving the city.

Those arms and those taken possession of when the news of the battle of Lexington first reached the city were used by the first troops raised in New York under the orders of Congress. The troops meeting with no other obstacle marched to the wharf arid embarked for Boston amid the hisses of an excited people. This prompt and decided action of the citizens struck dismay to the hearts of the adherents of the crown, gave them a foretaste of what might be expected, and at the same time, made the recruiting of troops for the colonies a much easier task.

By order of Congress, the colony of New York was required to raise four regiments, each to consist of ten companies and each company to be composed of some seventy-two men, making about 3,000 troops to be raised in New York. Of this number New York City was to raise one regiment. Each regiment was to be commanded by a colonel, a lieutenant-colonel and a major. Alexander McDougall was colonel of the first New York regiment, and young Willett was appointed second captain.

He received his appointment June 28, 1775. He was then in his thirty-fifth year, and as he says in his "narrative"; his health, strength, buoyancy of spirit and enthusiasm were his principal qualifications. His company was one of the first recruited and ready to take the field. Colonel Ethan Allen, the May preceding, had captured Ticonderoga in "the name of the Great Jehovah and the Continental Congress"; and this was considered the key to the gate way of Canada, and had much to do in turning the attention of Congress, Washington, General Schuyler and others in this direction, as the proper one for the invasion of that province.

There was a garrison of some 500 men at St. Johns on this route to Canada; another force at Chamblee, lower down the river, and some 300 tories and Indians at Montreal, which constituted about all of the effective troops of the British in Canada. It was believed all of these places and troops could be captured and Canada thereby prevailed upon to link its fortunes with the thirteen colonies.

On the 8th of August, 1775, Willett and his men took passage in a sloop up the Hudson, and reached Albany after a passage of four days. They were armed with the muskets which Willett had taken from the enemy, as before stated. At Albany this company was joined by three others, and there reviewed by General Montgomery, who was to accompany them.

Their destination was Canada, via Lake Champlain. They reached Ticonderoga in the course of two weeks, and were on the same grounds occupied by Willett when he was in the first battle seventeen years before. On the 29th of August 1,000 troops under Gen. Montgomery embarked in boats, proceeded down the lake, and on the 4th of September they were joined at Ile Aux Noix, at the foot of the lake, by Gen. Schuyler.

The 6th they proceeded to St. Johns, but found it too well fortified to take it by storm, with the small force and light guns of the Americans, and the next day they returned to the island. On the 10th of the month Gen. Montgomery, with 1,000 men, again proceeded to St. Johns, and landed just at dusk two miles from the fort. A detachment of 500 men, with which was young Willett, was sent below the fort to cut off the supplies of the enemy. This expedition, by reason of the bad conduct of the colonel in command, was unsuccessful, and again the troops returned to the island. Here they remained for a week.

When the American force was augmented to 2,000 men, and had received an additional supply of ammunition and larger guns, the army again embarked for St. Johns, under Gen. Montgomery, and late in the day landed at the place where the troops first disembarked. Again a detachment of 500 men was ordered below the fort, and this time Gen. Montgomery accompanied it, and it was successful in taking position and planting batteries. The siege slowly continued, large guns arrived and the garrison was severely annoyed. There was a fort at Chamblee, twelve miles from St. Johns, lower down the River Sorel, and on the route to Canada, garrisoned by about 170 men.

A detachment was sent to lay siege to that fort, and in less than two days, on October 18th, it surrendered with 168 men, seventeen cannon, six tons of powder. The colors of the seventh regiment were also captured and sent as a trophy to Congress. This capture was of great benefit to the besiegers of St. Johns. Nevertheless that garrison held out bravely, but on the 3d of November, after a siege of fifty days, that fort surrendered, and the prize was 500 regular troops and 100 Canadians (among whom were some of the French gentry) and a large quantity of military stores.

This was indeed a great success and was received by Congress and the country with feelings of delight; and well it might, for the troops were raw and undisciplined, the army supplies scant, the weather old and rainy, the grounds where the troops encamped damp and unhealthy, yet, in spite of all, a great victory was achieved. Capt. Willett was charged with the duty of escorting the prisoners to Ticonderoga, while Gen. Montgomery pushed on with an armed force to Montreal. As soon as the prisoners were safely placed in Fort Ticonderoga, Willett hastened to Montreal, and arrived there November 22, ten days after Montgomery had reached that place. The latter ordered Capt. Willett to return to St. Johns and take the command of that fort. This showed the high appreciation in which he was held by his superior officer.

Willett remained at St. Johns until in January, 1776, when the term of the enlistment of his troops having expired, he was relieved and again went to Montreal. On the 18th of February, by order of Gen. Montgomery, he left that place for Albany in charge of British officers and their families, and reached the latter place the last of the month. On the 1st of March he set out on horseback for New York, where he arrived the 5th.

The war having now assumed a severer aspect than was supposed fay many it would, it was found necessary to raise more troops with longer terms of enlistment. New York was required in 1776 to raise four battalions. Of the Third New York Regiment thus raised, Peter Gansevoort of Albany was appointed colonel and Marinus Willett lieutenant-colonel. The latter received his appointment the latter part of November, 1776, and with his appointment came orders to repair to Fishkill on the Hudson to recruit for his regiment. He was diligently employed there all winter in recruiting, drilling and clothing the men, and getting ready for the coming campaign.

At the opening of the spring of 1777, Col. Willett was ordered to take charge of Fort Constitution, opposite what is now West Point. It was so called because of the measures then being taken to form a state constitution for New York. During the whole war of the revolution it was a favorite scheme of the British government to obtain control of the Hudson, establish a chain of forts along that river and keep open a communication between New York City and Canada.

As soon as the ice was out of the Hudson, about the middle of March, 1777, sloops loaded with troops, started up that river to capture Forts Clinton and Montgomery and Peekskill. A body of troops landed at the latter place, set fire to the wharf and buildings, and made such a formidable demonstration as to cause the American commander at that port (Col. McDougall) to move the army stores to a place of safety, and his troops to the passes in the highlands, and to send to Col. Willett for help.

The express reached the latter on Sunday, March 23, while Col. Willett's men were out parading for a field review. The troops hurried to Peekskill and took post on an eminence that commanded a full view of the surrounding country. The practiced eye of Col. Willett noticed that a detachment of 100 men was separated from the main army of the enemy by a ravine, and he conceived the project of cutting them off and capturing the detachment; he took a circuitous route, crossed fences and other obstructions, but, as it was near dark and the detachment fled so precipitately to the shipping, he was unsuccessful. He captured, however, baggage, which had been left, consisting of blankets and cloaks; a blue camlet cloak, captured on that occasion, served afterwards to make the blue stripes to the flag that was first hoisted over Fort Stanwix, as will be hereafter narrated.

The enemy were thoroughly frightened and took refuge on board of the ships, weighed anchor, and by the light of the moon, the whole squadron swept down the Hudson back to the city. Col. Willett returned to Fort Constitution and there remained until May 18, when he was ordered to Fort Stanwix. He set out with his regiment in three sloops, and, in three days, reached Albany, thence up the Mohawk in boats, and arrived at Fort Stanwix, May 29, nineteen years later than his first visit under Gen. Bradstreet. Col. Gansevoort had preceded him in the arrival at that fort, and was chief in command.

In 1776 Washington saw the importance of Fort Stanwix, and wrote to Gen. Schuyler, in command of the northern frontier of New York, that Fort Stanwix should be put in repair and in a state of defense, but it seems, however, that but little was done. It was known early in the year 1777 that the British plan of the campaign for that year was for an army to enter New York via Lake Champlain, proceed to Albany, and to meet Gen. Howe, who was to go up the Hudson with his forces. It was to carry out that plan and to capture the forts on the Hudson that the incursion was made to Peekskill in March, 1777, as before stated. It was a part of the same plan for another force to proceed from Canada, via Oswego, Oneida Lake and Wood Creek, capture and garrison Fort Stanwix, proceed down the Mohawk, overrun the settlements of the valley and join the other British troops at Albany. This plan, if successful, would have been the death knell of American independence, as it would have separated the New England colonies from the other provinces and put the settlements of Tryon County at the mercy of the Tories.

When Col. Willett reached Fort Stanwix he found it was greatly out of repair; the ditch was filled up, the embankments crumbled away, the pickets had rotted down and the barracks and magazine gone to ruin. It is hardly worthwhile to relate in this connection the difficulties attending the repairs, the inefficiency, if not the culpable heedlessness, of the engineer in charge, a detection of his blunders by Col. Willett, and his arrest and dismissal to Gen. Schuyler at Albany, and the necessity of doing over again much of the work, and how it was not completed when the enemy arrived; all of these have been pretty fully narrated in the general, as well as the local history of the times.

About five P. M., August 2, bateaux loaded with supplies for the garrison and guarded by 200 men, reached the landing place on the Mohawk from down the river, and barely had time to get within the fort when an advance guard of sixty men of the enemy appeared in the skirt of the woods from the direction of Fort Bull. In fact, the captain had carelessly lingered behind and was taken prisoner. The garrison, by this 200 addition, consisted of 750 men, with six weeks provision, but a scanty supply of powder enough for six weeks if only nine cannon were fired each day. For a flag, this fort was up to that time without one.

The garrison heard, doubtless, in due time, in this far-off wilderness, the kind of flag Congress, on the 14th of June preceding, had adopted as the emblem of the nation that was to be, and, as necessity is the mother of invention, the troops devised the means for making a flag of the regulation style. For the white stripes shirts were cut up; to make the blue, the camlet cloak was used, captured by Col. Willett in March before, and for the red, old garments found by the garrison were improvised; some authorities say, the red was made from a petticoat, captured at the time of the camlet cloak. The army that was to come by way of Oswego, was under the command of Gen. St. Leger, of the regular army, and under him was Sir John Johnson in command of the Tories, and Brant in command of the savages about 1,000 in all. That force started from Montreal about June 21st, proceeded down the St. Lawrence, across Lake Ontario to Oswego, where it arrived about July 25th, and left the 28th for Oneida Lake, reaching the mouth of Wood Creek August 1st.

After the troops left Oswego, their progress was closely watched and daily reported to the garrison, by the friendly Oneidas, so that Col. Willett knew to a day when the army would arrive at Fort Stanwix. An advance guard of sixty men under Lieut. Bird were sent forward by St. Leger, to formally invest the fort, and that detachment arrived a little after five in the afternoon as heretofore stated.

On Sunday, August 3d, the remainder of the enemy reached the upper landing on Wood Creek (the site of the late United States arsenal) and there formed into line, to march with pomp and display over the intervening space to the fort. The day was bright and clear, and the pathway over the portage of sufficient width to enable the troops to show off to good advantage. The garrison were purposely paraded on the ramparts, not to fire, but to view the class of troops they were to meet, and to observe their movements and count their numbers. Not a gun was fired on either side.

The garrison simply watched and counted. The martial music was first heard, next came in sight the scarlet uniforms, and then the burnished firearms of the regular soldiers, the glittering tomahawks of the savages, and the wild feathers waving and tossing on their head gear. As they advanced the regular troops marched with precision and stately tread, deploying to the right and left, while the Indians spread out on the flanks, and with yells and war whoops made the forest resound with their reverberations, that drowned the sound of the bugle and the drum. In the midst of all, banners, ensigns and streamers floated to the breeze, and the whole display was intended to strike terror to the hearts of the garrison, but it had the opposite effect. They comprehended the situation, and saw the kind of foe they were to meet.

St. Leger placed a portion of his troops on the site of the late United States arsenal; another portion, with cannon and mortar with which to shell the fort, upon the rise of ground now occupied by St. Peter's Church. Sir John Johnson and his tories were stationed southeast of the fort, near the bend of the Mohawk, below where the railroad bridge now crosses that stream, and out of the reach of the guns of the fort, while the Indian camps were in the woods near the site now occupied by the railroad freight house; the river a few rods easterly, prevented the garrison from escaping in that direction. It will thus be seen how closely the investure was made, and how snugly the garrison was cooped up within the fortifications.

Very early on the morning of Monday, August 4, a brisk fire from the rifles of the Indians was commenced, which annoyed the garrison in their work on the parapets. The greater part of the 5th was occupied by both sides in firing at each other. Soon after dark of that evening the Indians spread themselves through the woods, completely encircling the fort, and almost the entire night kept up terrific yelling, so as to keep the garrison awake and on the *qui vive.*

Early on the morning of Wednesday, August 6, it was noticed that the Indian and Sir John Johnson's camps were nearly deserted, and that the enemy were stealthily stealing along the edge of the woods, on the south side of the river, toward Oriskany. The reason for this movement was not guessed by the garrison, for the Americans were not then aware that Herkimer was coming to their relief. About eleven in the forenoon two men sent by Gen. Herkimer two days before, succeeded in eluding the vigilance of the besiegers and in getting into the fort. They brought the news of Gen. Herkimer s approach, and it was then evident that the Indians and Tories had gone down the river to intercept the coming troops.

Then it was that Gen. Gansevoort resolved to make a sortie and attack the two camps that had been partially deserted. The men within the fort were paraded in a square, and the intelligence of Herkimer's coming was communicated to them. Col. Willett, who was to lead the sortie, went down into the esplanade and addressed the men substantially as follows: "Soldiers, you have heard that Gen. Herkimer is on his march to our relief. The commanding officer feels satisfied that the Tories and Queen's rangers have stolen off in the night with Brant and his Mohawks to meet him. The camp of Sir John is therefore weakened. As many of you as feel willing to follow me in an attack upon it, and are not afraid to die for liberty, will shoulder your arms and step out one pace in front."

Two hundred men obeyed the impulse almost at the same moment; fifty more with a three pounder were soon added. A rain storm nearly at that instant came up, which delayed the sortie until three P. M., but as soon as the storm ceased the men issued from the sally port at a brisk pace, and rushing down on Sir John Johnson's camp, near the bend of the river, below the present railroad bridge, carried it at the point of the bayonet, drove the enemy into and across the Mohawk at that point, and captured a large amount of army stores arid a number of prisoners, among whom was Col. Singleton, who was at the battle of Oriskany a few hours before, but had returned to camp in the meantime. He informed Col. Willett, as the latter states in his "narrative"; that Sir John was also in camp, and fled across the river. If this was correct information, Sir John must also have returned from Oriskany, for the reliable accounts show he was in that battle.

After Sir John's camp was scattered, Col. Willett turned his attention to the Indian camp, on or near the site of the present railroad freight house, and soon drove the Indians into the woods. When St. Leger, at his camp on the present site of St. Peter's Church, learned of the sortie he hurriedly crossed the Mohawk at that point and followed downstream to where "Factory Village"; now is, on the opposite side from the fort, with a view to cut off Col. Willett's return. St. Leger had two brass field pieces, and, partly concealed in a thicket on the east side of the river, he opened a brisk fire on Col. Willett's men, but the latter returned it so effectively that they soon put St. Leger's force to flight and returned to the fort without the loss of a single man.

Col. Willett captured twenty-one wagonloads of supplies, with five British flags, all of Sir John's papers, including his orderly book, and also letters from down the valley, which were being sent to the garrison from their friends, and which had been captured from Gen. Herkimer a few hours before, but which the enemy had not opened.

The following is what Col. Willett says in his "narrative" was done on his return to the fort: "The five flags taken from the enemy were hoisted on the flagstaff, under the Continental flag, when all the troops in the garrison, having mounted the parapets, gave three as hearty cheers as perhaps were ever given by the same number of men." That account by Col. Willett himself establishes the fact that a flag of the regulation kind, (as he calls it the Continental flag) as adopted by Congress, was raised on

Fort Stanwix as early as August 6, 1777. I have not seen in any historical work that a flag as ordered by Congress was raised within the thirteen colonies prior to that time.

In the afternoon of Thursday, August 7, a white flag from the enemy approached the fort, accompanied by three officers, with a request they might enter with a message from St. Leger. Permission was granted, and, according to custom, they were first blindfolded and then conducted into the dining-room, where the windows were darkened, candles lighted, the table spread with some light refreshments, and they were then received by Col. Gansevoort in the presence of his officers. The bandage was then removed from the eyes of the British officers and the principal speaker (Major Ancram) made known his errand, the purport of which was a demand of the surrender of the fort, accompanied by intimations that if surrendered the prisoners would be treated humanely, but if taken by force St. Leger would not hold himself responsible for the acts of cruelty of the Indians.

Col. Willett was deputed to reply in behalf of the garrison and no one had more fire or greater spirit or was better qualified to speak on that occasion. He looked Major Ancram full in the face and with an earnestness and emphasis that admitted of no mistake or equivocation said in substance: "This garrison is committed to our charge and we will take care of it. After you get out of the fort you may turnaround and look at its outside, but never expect to come in again unless you come a prisoner. I consider the message you have brought a degrading one for a British officer to send and by no means reputable for a British officer to carry. For my own part, I declare that before I would consent to deliver this garrison to such a murdering set as your army, by your own account consists of, I would suffer my body to be filled with splinters and set on fire, as you know has at times been practiced by such hordes of women and children killers as belong to your army."

These sentiments were re-echoed with applause by all officers present of the garrison. A cessation of hostilities for three days was agreed upon. As nothing had been heard from down the valley since the battle of Oriskany the garrison was getting uneasy. They needed more ammunition and might soon need provisions. It was discussed within the fort that if Col. Willett, who was very popular in the Tryon County settlements, could show himself there a spirit of enthusiasm would be awakened and they would rally to the relief of the fort.

Influenced by these considerations Col. Willett agreed to make the hazardous attempt to reach the people down the river. Accordingly, at ten o'clock at night, Sunday, August 10, he, accompanied by Lieut. Stockwell, a good woodsman, each armed with a spear eight feet long, as his only weapon, with no provisions but crackers and cheese in their pockets and a quart canteen of spirits, no baggage or blankets, stole silently out of the sally port, crossed the river by crawling on a log, and when on the opposite side of the stream, where "Factory Village"; now is, it was pitch dark and they in the middle of a thick forest. In rambling about they lost their way and bearings and became alarmed by the barking of a dog not far away.

They were near an Indian camp, some of the Indians having taken a position on that side of the river after the sortie of Col. Willett. They stood perfectly still by the side of a large tree, not venturing to move for hours and until the morning star appeared. They then took a northerly course and struck the Mohawk again not far from what is now known as "Ridge" two miles north of the fort. They kept close to the river, waded in it, and some of the way crossed over from one side to the other, so as to conceal their trail and not be followed. They pursued this course for several hours and then turned easterly to strike the settlements down the river. In those days the Indian path was south of the Mohawk and seldom, if ever, was there traveling in the pathless woods north of that stream; nevertheless when night came those two dare not strike a fire or a light, lest it might attract attention of prowling Indians; and so they camped in the thicket, without fire, light, blankets or covering.

At peep of day they were on their feet, although both were tired, lame and sore for the day's traveling, and night's chill, and Col. Willett's rheumatism, yet they kept on their journey, but steered more southerly, and about nine in the morning they struck a heavy windfall where were growing large patches of ripe black berries. From this luscious fruit and the crackers and cheese and spirits the two had a hearty breakfast. The sun and points of compass were observed and without other guides they struck Fort Dayton (now Herkimer village) about three in the afternoon, having traversed a distance of fifty miles through an unknown forest, crossing streams and morasses, climbing hills and surmounting many other obstacles. The general route those two traveled is indicated as above by Col. Willett's "narrative" it must have been northerly of Floyd Corners, through Trenton and into Russia, Herkimer County.

"Simm's Frontiersmen of New York" says that years before the revolution a hurricane began in the westerly part of Oneida County and swept through the forest in an easterly direction across the present towns of Camden and Trenton, entering Herkimer County at a place called the "dugway" in Poland, and continued onward through the towns of Russia, Salisbury and Norway extending a distance of fifty or sixty miles in length. Its breadth ranged from 60 to 100 rods and so great was its fury that almost every tree in its course was torn up by the roots. Its traces were visible for more than half a century afterward and a portion of the ground over which that tornado passed is called "the hurricane"; to this day.

It was doubtless in the track of that tornado Col. Willett found those patches of berries. Jones Annals of Oneida county, state, that in the month of that siege, a hurricane of tremendous power passed through Westmoreland from west to east its ravages extended from Oneida Lake to Cooperstown, half a mile and in some places a mile in width, prostrating the entire forest in its sweep; the severest effects were in that town. If both of those historical accounts of tornadoes are correct, there were two of them, six or seven years apart, passing over this county, one north and the other south of the Mohawk.

On the arrival of Col Willett and Lieut. Stockwell at Fort Dayton, it was ascertained that Gen. Schuyler had ordered a brigade of Massachusetts troops, stationed some ten miles above Albany, to the relief of Fort Stanwix, and that Gen. Arnold was to be in command. Having rested for one night, Col. Willett and Lieut. Stockwell started early the next morning for Albany, on horseback to meet the troops and interview Gen. Arnold.

The troops were met the same evening on their way. It was then learned that the First New York Regiment was also on its way to relieve the fort. On Saturday, August 16, Gen. Arnold and Col. Willett reached Fort Dayton, were the troops were assembled; on the way from Albany, Col. W. stopped to see Gen. Herkimer at his residence near Little Falls, who that day had his leg amputated by reason of the injury in the battle at Oriskany ten days before; the latter died next day after the amputation.

About the time that Col. Willett started down the valley for assistance, Walter N. Butler, a tory, who was in the battle of Oriskany, and was in the siege of Fort Stanwix, also went down to the Mohawk Settlements to rally his Tory friends. A number of them had assembled by appointment on Friday evening, August 15, at the house of one Shoemaker, one of the king s justices of the peace of Tryon County, there to be addressed by Butler. Shoemaker then resided at or near what is now Mohawk village, nearly opposite Herkimer village.

The garrison of Fort Dayton received news of the assemblage and a detachment was sent to surround the house and capture the inmates. When Butler was in the midst of his harangue, the detachment swooped down upon the assemblage, and captured the whole posse, consisting of six or eight soldiers, and as many Indians, besides a number of tories, among whom was an ignorant, half-witted fellow by the name of Han Yost Schuyler. Gen. Arnold at once ordered a court martial to try Butler and Schuyler as spies, for being found within the American lines. Col. Willett was appointed judge advocate; the two were convicted and sentenced to be executed. Gen. Arnold approved the sentence and ordered the execution to take place the next morning.

Through the intercession of friends, the sentence of Butler was respited and he sent to Albany as a prisoner. Through carelessness or treachery he subsequently escaped and fled to Canada, and for years thereafter was the greatest scourge, by reason of his temper and cruelties ever inflicted upon the County of Tryon, and his name has been handed down through history, as the worst hated, and most detested of all the tories of those times. As to Han Yost Schuyler, his brother and widowed mother strongly interceded in his behalf and as he was a well-known Tory and regarded by the Indians with a sort of superstition they always entertain toward such unfortunates, Gen. Arnold conceived the idea of using him to frighten away the besiegers at Fort Stanwix. That ruse and its success, have been so often told, that the story need not be repeated here; suffice it to say that by reason of the exaggerated stories Han Yost communicated to St. Leger, of the near approach of an overwhelming relieving force, the siege was abandoned August 22, and the besiegers hurriedly returned by the route they came 20 days before, leaving behind the bombardier asleep in the bomb proof, St. Leger's private writing desk, the tents of the soldiers, provisions, artillery, ammunition, the entire camp equipage, and large quantities of other stores.

Han Yost Schuyler fled with the fugitives as far as Oneida Lake; there he found means to leave them and to return to the fort, and apprise Col. Gansevoort of the ruse. This was the first notice the latter received of Gen. Arnold's approach, and explained why St. Leger had left in such haste.

At four o'clock of the afternoon of the next day, Gen. Arnold arrived with his men, and with four brass field pieces, banners displayed, drums beating, music playing, they marched into the fort amid the booming of cannon, the discharge of musketry and the cheers of the garrison. The successful defense of Fort Stanwix to which Col. Willett so largely contributed, affixed the seal to American independence.

Within two months thereafter, Burgoyne and his army laid down their arms on the field of Saratoga. Ticonderoga was abandoned, the British gave up the control of the Hudson and retreated down the river and New York was redeemed. These victories and others, commencing at that lone fortress in the then far off wilderness, sent a glow of joy throughout the thirteen colonies, and paved the way for France in less than four months thereafter to acknowledge our independence.

The British press spoke in the highest praise of Col. Willett's achievements, of his journey down the river through pathless woods in quest of succor. Congress voted him a sword, and the next October, one was sent him, accompanied by a copy of the resolution of Congress, and a complimentary letter from John Hancock, president of that body. That testimonial is now in the possession of a descendant of Col. Willett, and a description of it is furnished me as follows: "It is one of ordinary length, rapier kind, running to a sharp point, and of Damascus steel; the handle is gold, platina and other metal, and on it is this inscription, "Congress to Col. Willett Oct., 1777."

After St. Leger's retreat Col. Willett passed several months in comparative inactivity. He completed the unfinished works of Fort Stanwix, and drilled the troops stationed there. The last of September, Col. Gansevoort having returned to that fort, Col. Willett set out to visit his family at Fishkill, where he arrived October 4, the very day the British captured Forts Clinton and

Montgomery, and thereby obtained for a short time, control of the Hudson. Col. Willett remained for a while in that vicinity, assisting in the defense of the country about that river. That fall he visited the army under Washington, a dozen of miles from Philadelphia, and remained there until January, 1778, when he returned to Fort Stanwix. Wearied with this inactive and monotonous life, he set out in June, 1778, to join the army under Washington; on reaching Fishkill, he found there Gen. Gates, and on the 21st of that month, news came that the British had evacuated Philadelphia. As Gen. Gates had important information to communicate to Washington, Col. Willett was sent as the confidential messenger. He remained with the main army, and took part in the battle of Monmouth on the 28th of June, and continued with that army the rest of the year 1778.

The great campaign for the year 1779, was to be an invasion of the country in the western part of New York, occupied by the Onondaga, Cayuga and Seneca Indians. Those tribes had taken sides with the British, and from their territory many of the incursions into the Mohawk settlements were planned; their rich agricultural fields had afforded support to the armies, and to the Indian families, while the war was thus carried on against the colonists.

Those tribes possessed large cultivated fields, of great productiveness, also extensive gardens and orchards, and lived in frame houses, and had acquired some of the arts, and were in the enjoyment of many of the comforts of civilized life. They raised in profusion apples, pears, peaches, plums, melons, squashes, grapes, cranberries, beans and tobacco; corn was raised in large quantities; ears of that grain measured twenty-two inches in length; the first sweet corn ever seen in New England was carried thither from the country of the Six Nations by a soldier in his knapsack, during the war of the revolution. This Indian country included some fifty to sixty towns, all rudely built for those times.

Washington, Schuyler and others and Congress felt that a country which furnished so much aid and comfort to the enemy, should be as thoroughly devastated as had been the valley of the Mohawk. To accomplish that purpose, two armies, one under Gen. Sullivan was to proceed from Pennsylvania, to meet one another under Gen. Clinton at or near the junction of Tioga and Susquehanna rivers, below Newtown, now near Elmira, and thence proceed via Seneca and the other inland lakes into the heart of the Indian country of western New York.

In April of that year, and as a part of the same campaign, some 600 troops, in charge of Cols. Willett and Van Schaick, were ordered from Fort Stanwix to go down Wood Creek and into Oneida Lake to the Onondaga River, and thence into the country of the Onondagas, to lay their settlements waste, destroy their buildings and inflict the same kind of chastisement upon them that had been inflicted upon the white settlements.

This expedition started from Fort Stanwix April 18, and was gone six days, traveling 180 miles, and most effectually accomplishing the work it set out to perform. About a dozen villages, extending a distance of some ten miles along the valley of the Onondaga streams, were burned, grain, cattle and other property destroyed, the swivel of their council house disabled, and the destruction of the settlements rendered complete.

Alter this work Col. Willett returned to Canajoharie and then joined Gen. Clinton's army, for its destination to meet Gen. Sullivan. Four weeks Gen. Clinton was occupied in making the needed preparations; in August he and his army went overland to the head of Otsego Lake, the head waters of Susquehanna River, taking 200 boats from Canajoharie, each drawn by four horses, to that lake. The waters of the lake and river were raised by a dam, and the loaded boats were launched, to be carried down the river by the rushing waters. For the energy and ability displayed by Col. Willett in the part be took to start that flotilla, Gen. Clinton paid him a high compliment in a letter to Gen. Schuyler. The two armies of Gens. Sullivan and Clinton united, and on the 29th of August was fought the bloody and hotly contested battle of Newtown, in which the Indians under Brant and the Tories under Sir John Johnson and Col. John Butler were totally routed.

The enemy fought with desperation, for they were fighting for their homes, and they knew that defeat meant the desolation of their country and the destruction of their firesides. There was no battle and not much opposition after that. Sullivan s army, 5,000 strong, overran the entire hostile country and laid it waste, leaving hardly a green, living or movable thing on the whole track of the invaders. They found it a garden, but left it a desert. Over forty towns, which included 700 buildings, were burned to ashes, 160,000 bushels of corn were destroyed, elegant gardens laid waste, 1,500 bearing fruit trees leveled to the ground, cattle killed or driven off, and the inhabitants compelled to seek safety in flight. It broke the backbone of the Iroquois confederacy, from which it never recovered.

That campaign has passed into history as the "Sullivan's expedition". The ravages of the Indian country, made by that expedition, incited those hostile tribes and the Tories to retaliate in kind and to wreak their vengeance the next year upon the white settlements of Tryon County. After that expedition Col. Willett again returned to the main army and rendered himself useful in connection therewith.

In the winter of 1779-80 he led a detachment of 500 men, and with one field piece, crossed at night on the ice over to Staten Island and captured seventeen wagonloads of stores, which at that particular juncture were of great service to the troops. The same winter he led another expedition to Paulus Hook, (Jersey City), captured a redoubt and all of the cattle of the British. It was the celerity of Col. Willett's movements, the fertility of his resources and his untiring activity that rendered him such a valuable aid to the patriot cause and so much dreaded by the enemy. He was in that war to the Americans what Sheridan was to the North and Stonewall Jackson to the South in the recent civil war. Wherever he commanded he inspired the confidence and enthusiasm of his men, and they generally followed wherever he dared to lead.

During the year 1780 and while the Indians and Tories were committing terrible ravages in Tryon County, Col. Willett was with the main army in Westchester County, but nothing of importance occurred, so far as he was concerned. The County of Tryon during the first six years of the war, suffered more severely than any other extent of territory within the thirteen colonies. Within its borders more campaigns were performed, more battles fought, more people murdered and more dwellings burned than in any other section. The Board of Supervisors of that county, reported to the Legislature in December, 1780, that during the war 700 buildings had been burned, 354 families had abandoned their homes and removed from the country, 613 persons had deserted to the enemy, 197 had been killed, 121 taken captives, and 1,200 farms were uncultivated by reason of the enemy, and this did not include some five or six other settlements.

Other statistics show that thousands of horses and cattle had been killed or stolen, millions of bushels of grain destroyed, and that 300 women had been made widows, and 2,000 children made orphans. These ravages and misfortunes, earned for the valley of the Mohawk, the title of "the dark and bloody ground", and well-nigh extinguished the hopes and crushed out the spirit of the people.

The year 1781 opened gloomily upon the inhabitants of that valley. In this emergency, Gov. Clinton bethought himself of one who could revive the drooping spirits of the people, whose presence would arouse great enthusiasm and be a tower of strength in the valley. That one was Col. Marinus Willett. At the urgent solicitation of Gov. Clinton and with great reluctance, Col. Willett consented to leave the main army, and make his headquarters in the valley to take command of the levies assigned to that branch of the State service. His strong sympathies with the suffering people, his acquaintance with Indian methods and modes of war fare, and the assurances of Gov. Clinton that his presence was needed, induced him to undertake the laborious and hazardous service. He has left on record the assertion that one year of such work was more trying and laborious than all of the other years of the war. The fore part of July, 1781, Col. Willett established his headquarters at Canajoharie, and it was not long thereafter before his services were called into requisition.

In the year 1781 there were twenty-four forts between Schenectady and Fort Dayton, (now Herkimer village), into which the inhabitants of the valley sought refuge when pressed by the enemy, or otherwise threatened with danger. Some of these forts were nothing more than dwellings within picketed inclosures; nevertheless they afforded a comparative security against sudden irruptions from the foe.

Early that year the whole northern and western frontiers of New York were threatened with invasions, and the people were weighed down by a deeper feeling of unrest and despondency than at any former period during the war. The country between Albany and Lake Champlain was suffering for want of provisions and in danger of raids from Canada in that direction, while Brant and his dusky warriors were hovering about the valley of the Mohawk, ready to pounce upon any soldier or inhabitant who was unfortunate enough to be caught away from his comrades or the forts.

It was in the spring of that year that Brant and his Indians, while prowling around Fort Stanwix and its vicinity, picked up and carried off some thirty of the garrison of that fort.

In May of the same year that Fort was so badly injured by fire and flood that it was abandoned, and the men removed to other quarters. It was in the midst of this deep gloom and general discouragement that Col. Willett consented to take command of the northwestern frontier and make his headquarters in the

Mohawk valley. The fore part of July, 1781, he established himself at Canajoharie, where he had one hundred and twenty men; at Fort Herkimer he had about twenty more, at Ballston some thirty, and at Catskill twenty; in other parts of the valley were less than one hundred more. These did not include the militia nor the new levies soon expected to be raised. The country he was to defend was all of New York west of Albany county, and included Catskill and other -exposed points along the Hudson. He was not left long without occupation; even while establishing his headquarters, a force of three or four hundred, mostly Indians, was on its way from Canada to attack the Mohawk settlements. Capt. John Dockstador was a bitter Tory, and, some time before, had fled from that part of the country and collected the above Indians and Tories to return and raid his old neighbors and acquaintances, and in hopes, if successful, of becoming a major.

This raiding party took the route from Canada, through the Seneca country, traveled by the "Sullivan expedition"; of two years before, thence struck off for the head waters of the Susquehanna to the Mohawk valley settlements, in the direction of what is now Sharon Springs. Dockstader and his men, pursued their course with such quietness and stealth, that they reached without being discovered, a dense cedar swamp of some seventy-five acres, about half a mile southwest of what is now Sharon Centre, some two miles east of Sharon Springs.

Upon a slight rise of ground within that swamp, concealed from view, those raiders encamped for the first night, and most of them started off the next morning, Monday, July 9th, to attack Corrytown, a small settlement of a dozen houses, six or eight miles distant in a northeasterly direction, in what is now the town of Root, in Montgomery county, three miles south of Spraker's Basin, and about a dozen miles southeasterly from Canajoharie, where Col. Willett was located.

It so happened that early on the same morning, that those Indians and Tories left that swamp for Corrytown, Col. Willett, without knowing that an enemy was in that direction, sent out from Canajoharie, a scouting party of thirty-five men, under Capt. Gross, to patrol the country around Sharon Springs, then a strong Tory settlement known as New Dorlach, and to procure beeves and other supplies for the garrison, also to see if an enemy was near.

The fact that New Dorlach was a Tory settlement, was doubtless the incentive for Dockstader, to make that swamp his headquarters and hiding place, for his Tory sympathizers were undoubtedly apprised of his coming, and kept it a secret. The same feeling probably moved Col. Willett to be suspicious of that locality, and to make it the base of his supplies.

Capt. Gross had been gone but a few hours on his scouting expedition, when the garrison at Canajoharie, discovered about noon, fire and smoke in the direction of Corrytown. The Indians had commenced their work of pillage and destruction. Col. Willett at once dispatched to Corrytown, Capt. McKean, with sixteen levies and with orders to collect as many militia on the route, as he could gather, and at the same time he sent a messenger post haste after Capt. Gross to inform him of the fire, and of the probable proximity of the enemy in New Dorlach, with instructions to discover their location.

Capt. Gross struck the trail the enemy made, when it left the swamp for Corrytown, and by its width, estimated the number to be three or four hundred; he sent two or three of his men to follow the trail to its starting place, while he retired to a safe and convenient point of observation, and waited for his men to return; after following the trail about a mile, the men reached the encampment in the swamp, discovered a large number of packs, and that some of the Indians left behind were engaged in cooking, as if expecting the main body to return for the night.

They, undiscovered, stole a blanket from one of the tents and then hurried back to report to Capt. Gross. The latter at once sent a man on horseback to Col. Willett. In the meantime the latter was busy all the afternoon in collecting the militia and getting ready to start at a moment's notice.

Capt. McKean reached Corrytown in time to quench the flames in one or two of the dwellings after the enemy had left, but not in time, nor would he have been able had he arrived sooner, to save the dozen other buildings, which Dockstader and his men burned to the ground, nor to have protected the inhabitants, which were murdered or carried away captives by that superior force. There was a picketed block house in that settlement into which a few hurried and were saved, while others sought safety by hiding in the woods, or by being fleet of foot. Cattle and horses were killed or driven away, and, when the Indians left, about 4 P. M., they left behind them a sad and sickening scene of desolation.

When word from Capt. Gross reached Col. Willett it was near night, and he at once set off for the swamp, with orders for Capt. McKean and Capt. Vedder at Fort Paris (two miles northeast of Fort Plain) to follow. It was Col. Willett's intention to reach the camp in the night, surprise and attack it before daylight, but the woods were thick, with no road better than a bridle path; the night was dark, and the guide lost his way, so that it was six in the morning before Col. Willett and Capts. McKean and Gross reached the camp.

In the meantime the enemy had news of the approach and had changed their ground to a more advantageous position, about one-eighth of a mile northwest of Sharon Centre, instead of one-half a mile to the southwest, where they encamped. Col. Willett divided his forces into two parallel lines, or in the form of a crescent and placed them in a ravine and sent a small detachment over the brow of the hill to show themselves to the enemy with orders at the first tire to retreat and draw the Indians into the ravine much like the trap into which Herkimer was caught at the battle of Oriskany.

The decoy succeeded and the Indians came rushing on, yelling, whooping, hallooing, until they met Col. Willett's men;

there they were checked, the tide of battle turned, and after a sharp fight of nearly two hours, the enemy fled, Col. Willett following vigorously in the pursuit, calling on his men to follow, while he waved his hat and shouted at the top of his voice, "Come on boys, the day is ours. I can catch in my hat all the bullets the rascals can send", and at the same time, gave orders in a loud tone of voice, as if directing a detachment to reach the rear of the enemy to cut off their retreat. The Indians and Tories were thoroughly frightened and fled in great confusion, leaving behind the plunder and booty taken the day before, killing some of their captives and hurrying off with the rest. They also left behind forty of their own dead and all of their camp equipage.

The victory was complete, and produced inspiriting effect upon the Americans. The loss of Col. Willett was five men, among whom was the brave and meritorious Capt. McKean and his son. The captain was shot in the battle, but died after he had reached Canajoharie. Dockstader and his men hurriedly left the valley, he without earning the commission of major, which he expected, and that party did not again molest the Mohawk settlements.

A brief sketch of some of the incidents attending this invasion will be sufficient to indicate the trials and sufferings the inhabitants of Tryon county passed through during the whole period of the revolutionary war. The attack upon Corrytown was so wholly unexpected the settlers were not prepared for it, most of them were at work in the fields, and but few had an opportunity to reach the picketed inclosure. Jacob Diefendorf, a pioneer settler, with his two young sons, were at work in the field; one of the sons, 12 or 14 years old, was tomahawked and scalped, and after lying several hours insensible, bathed in his blood, he crawled to the picketed enclosure, without knowing what he was doing. On reaching his friends he imploringly raised his hands and besought them not to kill him; his wounds were dressed, and he recovered and lived for several years thereafter. The other son was taken captive and carried to the cedar swamp, and when the

Indians were routed by Col. Willett, young Diefendorf was scalped and left for dead. He covered himself with the leaves of the trees to keep off the flies from his wound, and when discovered, covered and begrimed with blood, he was at first supposed to be an Indian. He was taken back to his friends, his wounds dressed, and, although his head was five years in healing, he eventually recovered and became one of the wealthiest farmers in Montgomery County. He died in 1859 at the age of 85 years.

A girl a dozen years old, was also taken prisoner to that cedar swamp, and when the enemy were defeated and found they could not take their young captive with them to Canada, the Indians took her scalp, as they did not wish to lose the bounty the British government had offered for scalps. When the settlers at Corrytown saw the enemy approaching, a husband and father started from his house with his family to reach the picketed block house. He had a small child in one hand and his gun in the other, followed by his wife with an infant in her arms and several children on foot hold of her dress. A savage fired at them, the bullet passed near the head of the child in the father's arms and lodged in the pickets. That was the last family that reached the fort. As before stated, the Indians plundered all of the buildings in the neighborhood and set them on fire, and all were burned except one.

The news of Dockstader's defeat was received with great joy throughout the country. The common council of the city of Albany, on the 19th of the month the battle was fought, passed complimentary resolutions in favor of Col. Willett and his officers and men for their bravery and intrepidity in that battle and voted to Col. Willett the freedom of that city. That battle took place on July 10, 1781, and has passed into history as "the battle of Sharon". Its centennial anniversary was observed in July, 1881, by the inhabitants of that part of the State.

As I learn from residents of that locality that cedar swamp yet remains, covered with trees, about as impassable as ever, except in very dry seasons or in the coldest of weather, when the grounds and the small lake in the center are frozen hard. Soon after that battle news came to Col. Willett at one o'clock at night that a party of fifty or sixty-Indians were hovering around a settlement five or six miles distant. In an. hour s time he had a captain of militia company, with seventy men, in pursuit, but the Indians wisely took to their heels. It was by reason of such promptness and the celerity of Col. Willett's movements, his dash in battle, and his seeming ubiquity that the Indians had such a dread and fear of him; they believed he possessed supernatural powers; they called him, "the devil".

During that summer the enemy appeared at intervals in small numbers in different parts of the valley, but nothing occurred to dignify it with the name of an invasion or a raid.

Over three months had passed since the irruption of Dockstader; the farmers had gathered their crops, filled their granaries, and partially settled down into the belief that the year 1781 would pass along without any more formidable invasions of the valley, with its attendant consequences. If such a hope was entertained, it proved illusory, and the expectation was doomed to disappointment. In the forenoon of Wednesday, October 24th, a hostile force of 700 men, composed of British, Indians and Tories under the command of Majors Ross and Walter N. Butler was first discovered in the valley near Argusville in Schoharie County, making its way towards Corrytown.

That expedition was organized at Bucks, now called Carleton Island in the St. Lawrence, and thence it proceeded across Lake Ontario to Oswego, thence by the water route to Oneida Lake as far as Chittenango Creek; at that point, the boats were secreted, and the men struck across the country through Onondaga, Madison and Otsego counties, to the vicinity in Schoharie, where first discovered. The enemy proceeded to Corrytown, plundered the dwellings, made prisoners of the inhabitants, but avoided setting fires, lest they might alarm the garrison of Col. Willett, and thereby be frustrated in accomplishing their undertaking. From that point they proceeded to the Mohawk, followed it down on the south side, to Fort Hunter, where Schoharie Creek empties into the river; they arrived at that point at nightfall, crossed over the creek into what was then called Warrensburgh, now the town of Florida in Montgomery County. Fearing they were going too far to the eastward, they crossed the next morning to the northerly side of the Mohawk, cast of Tribe's Hill, and by a circuitous route went to Johnstown and the old baronial hall of Sir William Johnson, where they arrived at noon Thursday, October 25th.

The whole track of the enemy was marked by the murder or capture of inhabitants, stealing of horses and cattle, plunder of dwellings and destruction of property. Late in the afternoon of the day the enemy was seen moving down the river towards Fort Hunter, the news of their march was brought to Col. Willett; he immediately mustered all the spare forces at hand, sent orders to other points for the militia to follow on after him, while he crossed to the south side of the Mohawk in pursuit. He marched all night, and reached Fort Hunter, some twenty miles east of Canajoharie, in the morning, and was proceeding to cross Schoharie Creek, and follow the enemy into the town of Florida, when he learned that the latter was on their way to Johnstown.

The Mohawk was deep at that point and not fordable and Col. Willett was obliged to procure boats or floats to get his men over that river, so that it was noon before he reached the north side. His troops were at once formed in marching order and set off in haste for Johnstown. Col. Willett had 416 men; the enemy about double that number. They reached Johnstown about the middle of the afternoon. Col. Willett sent a small detachment under command of Major Rowley to the east to attack the enemy in the rear, while he engaged them in front. A sharp engagement ensued, resulting in driving the enemy into the edge of the woods nearby, when of a sudden, without any known or explainable reason, Willett s men were seized with a panic and fled from the field, leaving a cannon in possession of the enemy, and some of them seeking refuge in a stone church.

The efforts of Col. Willett to rally them were in vain. At that unfortunate time Major Rowley s force came upon the enemy's rear, attacked them with great vigor, throwing them into confusion and driving them from the field. They, however, rallied, and in turn drove back Major Rowley, and the two contending forces were alternately defeated, and so the fighting continued until sunset. In the meantime Col. Willett succeeded, in gathering his men and returned to the fight.

At dark the enemy was totally beaten, driven further into the woods, and sought safety on the top of a mountain, six miles distant to the north. After dark Col. Willett procured lights and buried the dead. His loss was forty killed; he took fifty prisoners, from whom it was learned that the enemy intended to move the next day upon Stone Arabia, in the vicinity of what is now known as Palatine Bridge, with a view to obtain provisions. Col. Willett moved his men to that locality, while he sent a scouting party to follow the enemy and keep track of their movements. By this scouting party he learned that the enemy were moving north to westerly, nearly parallel with the Mohawk, toward the northerly part of Herkimer county, as if it was the intention to get out of the reach of the Americans, and then strike down to the Mohawk and across the country to Chittenango Creek, where the boats had been left.

To prevent such a movement, Col. Willett, on the morning of Saturday, October 27, sent a detachment to destroy the boats while he marched his men to Fort Herkimer, on the south side of the river, some two miles east of Herkimer village, there to await developments, still keeping spies on the trail of the enemy, with orders to send swift messengers to him at every turn of affairs. Majors Ross and Butler marched their men at a slow pace, for they were hemmed in the woods, short of provisions, and exposed to great dangers. On Monday, October 29, they encamped in a thick wood in the north part of what is now the town of Norway, about half a mile from Black Creek an encampment which has passed down by traditions as "Butler's ridge".

Thus it will be seen, by looking on a map of New York, the slow progress that was made after the battle of Johnstown, some forty miles distant. During the four days the enemy was on that route the weather was cold and each man had only one-half pound of horse flesh each day on which to subsist. On the 28th the detachment returned, which Col. Willett had sent to the boats, without having accomplished (for some reason,) the work it was sent to do.

Late in the afternoon of Sunday, October 28, Col. Willett received word that the enemy were striking still deeper into the wilderness, as if to make their escape by crossing West Canada Creek miles above Trenton Falls, and thence steer their course through a pathless forest, via the Black River to Carleton Island. To frustrate that move, a short time before dark of the same day, Col. Willett selected 400 of his best troops with sixty Oneida Indians, who had that day joined his forces, and taking five days provisions, he started out, crossed the Mohawk, and followed up the valley of West Canada Creek and encamped that night in the woods above Fort Dayton (now Herkimer village).

Early the next morning, Col. Willett and his men were astir, following up the easterly side of the creek, to what is now Middleville, marching in the midst of a driving snow storm, and pushing their way in a northeasterly direction, into the north part of the town of Norway, and at dark, encamped for the night in a dense wood, about a mile, as it turned out, from the enemy's encampment. A scouting party was at once sent forward to discover the location of the foes, and to ascertain whether Col. Willett was in their front or rear that party soon returned with the news of the proximity of the retreating forces, and at first, Col. Willett thought to make a night attack, but as the enemy had a supply of bayonets which his men had not, he concluded to wait until the morrow.

At break of day, Tuesday, October 30, the Americans were again on foot, a scout having been sent ahead to learn what the enemy were doing. The main body of the men of Ross and Butler were up as early as the pursuers and on the march, a detachment being in the rear as a guard, and to bring on the baggage and provisions; that scouting party got in between the advance and rear forces, and one of them was shot while the others hurried back to Willett with the news.

The pursuers were hurriedly pushed forward, and overtook the enemy near Black Creek, an engagement ensued, in which the enemy were compelled to retreat; frequent skirmishes took place all the way to West Canada Creek, some two or three miles, the enemy seeming perfectly discouraged and demoralized and only too anxious to get out of reach and harm s way.

They reached West Canada Creek, hurriedly crossed, and when on the opposite shore rallied and another sharp skirmish ensued the creek separating the combatants. In that engagement Walter N. Butler was shot and instantly killed, as Col. Willett says, the ball entered his eye and passed out the back part of his head.

Accounts differ as to whether Butler was killed by a random shot, or by one taking deliberate aim, and also as to whether he was scalped. The most reliable account is, that he was killed by a stray bullet and that he was not scalped, as Col. Willett makes no mention of it in his narrative, but simply says, "he was shot dead." Thus perished Walter N. Butler, the greatest scourge, the most cruel and in human monster, and the worst hated Tory, who inflicted his presence upon the border settlements of Pennsylvania and New York.

His father later on offered a reward for the recovery of the body, but it was never restored to him, nor would the American soldiers accord it a burial; they left it to bleach and rot upon the identical ground where it had fallen. The news of this victory and death spread through the valley, about the time that the tidings came of the capture of the army of Cornwallis at Yorktown: yet that surrender did not give more, if so much, joy to the inhabitants of the valley, as the assurance that Walter Butler had passed from earth.

After the shooting of Butler the enemy fled in confusion, and at a rapid gait, leaving behind packs and all that encumbered their retreat, and struck off through the dense and pathless wilderness in the direction of the valley of the Black River. After seven days journey, of innumerable sufferings and untold hardships, they reached Carleton Island, eighty miles distant, in a famishing condition, many of the men who crossed Canada Creek having perished by the way.

Col. Willett and his men crossed that stream and followed in pursuit until nearly dark; but as the Americans were getting short of provisions, and as the enemy retreated with such rapidity, it was deemed prudent to return, as the victory was as complete as if the whole of the enemy s forces were captured.

On the return to recross the creek, the Americans discovered a five-year-old white girl near a fallen tree, crying piteously. She had been stolen from her parents, but as the Indians did not wish to be further encumbered with her, they left the waif where she was found, near the fallen tree. The little girl was taken in charge and restored to her friends down the valley.

The place of the enemy's crossing on West Canada Creek is about five miles up the stream from Gang, or Hinkley's Mills, and nearly double that distance above Trenton Falls. It is near the line between the towns of Russia and Ohio in Herkimer County. At that point the stream is fordable for two or three miles, owing to the rifts and to small and large stones in the channel of the creek. It is now known as "Hess's Rifts", and the crossing place is called by some "Butler's Ford". In the pocket of Butler when his dead body was found was the same commission he exhibited on his trial as a spy four years before at the time Col. Willett acted as judge advocate some ten days after the battle of Oriskany. Let me state in this connection and by way of parenthesis that Dr. William Petry (grandfather of Judges Robert and Samuel Earl of Herkimer,) was surgeon general in Col. Willett's regiment, appointed in April, 1781, and was in this expedition ; and was all through the war, and was wounded at the battle of Oriskany four years before.

The loss of the enemy in this October incursion of Ross and Butler was never known. Col. Willett s official dispatches contain the following: "The fields of Johnstown, the brooks and rivers, the hills and mountains, the deep and gloomy marshes and dense woods through which they had to pass, these only could tell; and perhaps the officers who detached them on this expedition." Gen. Heath, the American commander of the northern frontier, issued a general order in November, 1781, commending Lord Sterling, Gen. Stark and others for their services that year, and mentions the battle of Johnstown, the defeat of Ross and Butler and the death of the latter, and adds: "The general presents his thanks to Col. Willett whose address, gallantry and persevering activity exhibited on this occasion do him highest honor."

This expedition closed the war in the valley of the Mohawk for that year. In fact, there was no longer much of anything left in that valley for a hostile expedition to destroy; the inhabitants had lost pretty much all, except the soil they cultivated, most of their fine farms had been turned into a wilderness waste, except in the vicinity of the forts, and at times hunger stared the settlers in the face, and famine seemed inevitable.

These resistances in the valley, may seem unimportant, because no great battles were fought, and no great victories won; nevertheless they stemmed the tide of the enemy s advance into the interior, and kept them back from the towns of the Hudson, and prevented the establishment of a chain of forts along that river, which was a favorite scheme and a long cherished hope and object of the British. For the year 1782, Col. Willett remained at his headquarters on the Mohawk, but no considerable force of the enemy appeared at any one time, to molest the inhabitants of Tryon County. Small and scattering bodies of Indians appeared at various places, causing trouble and creating alarm, but no very serious disturbances occurred.

The exigencies of the times required vigilance and alertness on the part of Col. Willett, and the sending of squads of troops in the night, several miles into the wilderness, or into neighboring localities, to drive out the enemy, or to discover if one was near, yet the campaign of 1782 closed without any important event in Tryon county. The substantial fighting of the war ended with the surrender of Cornwallis, and negotiations for peace between the two countries were commenced in Europe near the close of the year of 1782.

For nearly a year there was an armistice, nevertheless, none of the efforts of the American officers were relaxed, to preserve the discipline of the troops and to keep the country in an attitude of defense. The recruiting of New York State troops had been successful that year, by reason of the legislature offering a bounty of money, instead of a bounty in lands, so that at the close of the year 1782, Col. Willett had a regiment of 400 State troops. Having prepared winter barracks for his men, inoculated many of them for small pox, and built a log hut for himself, Col. Willett set out the last of November for Albany. Thence he went to Fishkill for his wife, with the intention to take her to his winter quarters during the winter of 1782-3.

At that time Gen. Washington's headquarters were at Newburgh, opposite Fishkill Landing, and there Col. Willett went to pay his respects to the Commander-in-chief; he remained to dinner, and as he left the table and arose to depart, Washington invited Col. Willett into the office, and unfolded a secret plan of sending an expedition the then coming winter to surprise and capture Oswego. Col. Willett was asked to lead the expedition. The latter had made arrangements for passing the winter with his wife in comfortable quarters, and it was with reluctance that he hesitated to accept the request of the commander in-chief. He departed with a promise to think of it and let Washington soon know the result of his conclusions. A correspondence ensued, and as Gen. Washington desired to keep the matter a profound secret, the correspondence on his part was in his own handwriting. Col. Willett accepted the position.

At that time Oswego was one of the most formidable defenses on this continent, and had given the enemy by its possession, and that of Niagara, great advantage during the war. The whole expedition was to be one of secrecy, for upon it depended its success, and the positive instructions of Washington to Col. Willett were, not to attack nor attempt to capture Oswego, except by surprise.

On Saturday, the 8th of February, 1783, the troops were suddenly assembled at Fort Herkimer, and a large portion of them supplied with snow shoes, as they had no beaten track to follow, and the snow was from two and one-half to three feet deep. The men thus provided went ahead and made a track for a cavalcade of 200 sleighs that followed, carrying the remainder of the troops and the baggage.

The expedition reached Oneida Lake Sunday night, February 9, and crossed it that night on the ice, and arrived at Fort Brewerton, at the foot of the lake, where the sleighs were left, and the men followed the river on ice to Oswego Falls (now Fulton) and arrived there about 2 p. M., February 10. There they went into the woods, made ladders and the prospect of stealing unawares upon the garrison and capturing the fort was everything that could be desired.

At 10 O'clock that night the expedition reached a point of land about four miles from the fort; here on account of the weakness of the ice on Oswego River, men were obliged to take to the land, and pursue the route through the woods. An Oneida Indian, who was considered every way trustworthy and reliable, and supposed to be familiar with the woods and the route, was selected as a guide. Four hours remained before the moon set, the time appointed to attack the fort, then four miles distant.

The guide took the lead, the men following his track. In two hours' time, not discovering an opening in the woods, Col. Willett went to the front to ascertain the cause, and learned the guide was considerably ahead and the men following blindly on the tracks in the snow; in the course of an hour the guide was overtaken and found standing still, apparently lost and bewildered. The men had been led into a swamp, some in sunken holes and many had frozen feet and one man was frozen to death. The guide had struck other tracks in the snow, which he followed supposing they led to the fort, but instead, they led in another direction down the lake.

In this perplexity there was no alternative but to forego the attack on the fort, and to retrace their steps. The men were in the woods three days without provisions, and were gone twelve days on the expedition. Before they left Fort Herkimer peace had been concluded in Europe, but it was not known in this country; while this expedition was on its way to Oswego, the news of peace was received by Congress.

After Col. Willett returned to his headquarters he went to Albany and there heard the glorious news proclaimed to the rejoicing inhabitants by the town clerk at the city hall. In Col. Willet's "narrative", the letters to him from Gen. Washington in relation to that expedition, are published, and the one of March 5, 1783, completely exonerates him from all blame and expresses the high sense which the commander-in-chief entertained of Col. Willett's persevering exertions and zeal on that expedition, and tendered his warmest thanks on the occasion.

On Friday, April 11. 1783, Congress issued its proclamation announcing a cessation of hostilities on sea and land, and once again smiling peace prevailed throughout the borders. The thirteen colonies were now a free and independent nation, the armies were disbanded, the soldiers returned to the peaceful pursuits of life, exchanged the weapons of war for the implements of husbandry, the scattered population of the country gradually gathered at their firesides, at their old homes, and once more the people of Tyron county rejoiced and smiled through their tears.

And now was to follow the inauguration of a new government, the adoption of a new civil polity and the creation of new offices. Old things were to be done away and all things to become new. There was a general hatred of everything that was English, and a universal feeling that, as far as possible, it should be banished from the land. The name of Kings College was changed to that of Columbia.

The county of Charlotte, named in honor of England s queen, the wife of George III, of revolutionary times, was, by an act of the legislature of April, 1784, changed to that of Washington; while by the same act of the legislature, and as a grateful tribute and sense of poetic justice, the county named after the hated and last Tory governor of New York, the county wherein Col. Willett achieved his grandest triumphs, was given the name of the patriot, Montgomery, under whom Capt. Willett won his first laurels in battling for the existence of the infant republic. These are but a few instances of the changes effected. So, too, those who had served faithfully and honorably in the war, were generally remembered and rewarded in the civil appointments in the State, although no law was passed, as there was 100 years later, requiring such appointments to be preferential.

Col. Samuel Clyde, a major at the battle of Oriskany, and who had rendered efficient services in the Mohawk valley as an officer in the American army, was appointed the first sheriff of Montgomery county, Col. Colbrath, another officer in the patriot army, and lieutenant in the "Sullivan expedition", was appointed the first sheriff of Herkimer, and later, the first one of Oneida. Col. Willett was elected to the assembly from New York in 1783, and the next year appointed sheriff of that county for three years.

To be "high sheriff" was considered in those times of more importance, dignity and consequence than in these days to be governor of the State. The grandfather of Col. Willett was sheriff of Queens County in 1820, and his ancestors, sheriffs of that county as follows: Thomas Willett in 1683, Elbert in 1705, Thomas in 1707, Cornelius in 1708 and Thomas in 1770.

In 1790 Col. Willett was appointed by President Washington commissioner to the Creek Indians, on a peace mission, that tribe having assumed a hostile attitude. He left in March and was absent four months, and was eminently successful in his errand, and war was averted. Col. Willett's thorough acquaintance with Indian character, habits, modes of thought and reasoning, peculiarly fitted him for such a mission.

In 1791 he was again appointed sheriff of New York, and held the office this time for four years.

Col. Willett was of powerful frame and of great physical strength, and, of course, perfectly fearless. It is stated that while sheriff, to quell a riotous assemblage, he collared the ringleader, a brawny, broad shouldered, two-fisted butcher, and laid his prostrate form, on the floor, where he was held as power less as a hoppled sheep.

In 1792 Col. Willett was elected one of the directors of the Western Inland Lock Navigation Canal, the object being internal improvements, to connect the waters of the Hudson with Lakes George and Champlain and those of the Mohawk with Wood Creek at Rome. In the same year a general Indian war with the western tribes was apprehended, and Col. Willett was tendered the office of brigadier general in the United States army.

This position he declined as he was not in favor of thus dealing with the Indians; his advocacy of peace policy was adopted and war avoided. In 1807 he was appointed mayor of New York in place of DeWitt Clinton and was, a year later, succeeded by Mr. Clinton. That office in those times of Col. Willett was one of great honor, dignity and emolument, and was sought after by men of ability and high standing. It is said to have been worth from $10,000 to $15,000 a year, and Col. Willett said that office yielded him a greater revenue during the year he held it, than did the seven years office of sheriff. In 1803 when DeWitt Clinton was first appointed to that office, he resigned the office of United States Senator to accept it, and he had for his competitors Edward Livingston, Morgan Lewis, then Justices of the Supreme Court of the State, and the next year elected Governor.

The great-grandfather of Col. Willett, it will be remembered, was the first English mayor of New York. In 1811 DeWitt Clinton was the nominee for the office of lieutenant-governor of one branch of his party, and Col. Willett of the other branch.

Col. Nicholas Fish, of the army of the revolution, father of Hamilton Fish, afterward governor, was the Federal nominee. The latter received an overwhelming majority in New York city as the opponents of Mr. Clinton, in his own party, voted direct for Mr. Fish, as the surer way of defeating Mr. Clinton. But the latter was elected, as he was strong in the rural districts. Hammond's Political History of New York, in referring to this contest, says that Col. Willett had been an officer of great merit in the revolutionary war, and in private life was regarded as an amiable and worthy citizen, but he had been somewhat wavering in politics and, in former days, had been inclined to support the faction of Aaron Burr.

In the war of 1812 an immensely large public meeting was held in City Hall Park in August, 1814, to support that war and approve the measures of President Madison. Col. Willett addressed that meeting and, while standing beneath the flag of the nation, which waved over his head, he made a brief, but telling speech, which awakened unbounded enthusiasm and applause. He said it was a favorite toast in the war of the revolution that "May every citizen become a soldier, and every soldier a citizen"; and that the time had again come when our citizens must be soldiers. He concluded his brief speech as follows: " In the war of the revolution there was a chorus to a song we used to sing in camp, in days of much more danger, which ran as follows:

Let Europe empty all her force,
We'll meet them in array
And shout Huzza, Huzza, Huzza.
For life and liberty.

This pithy discourse from an old man, near seventy-five years of age, whose services in behalf of his country were well known, was applauded to the very echo. In the Greek revolution of 1823 Col. Willett warmly sympathized with the oppressed of that country. He was chairman of a committee appointed to aid the Greeks in their struggle for in dependence. A large meeting was held in the park in New York City, which was addressed by Col. Willett.

In that speech, he referred to the fact that it was in the same place, where he assisted in 1765 in burning effigies of those who aided in the passage of the odious stamp act; the same park, where enthusiastic meetings were held in 1775, in favor of American independence in which he took part; that those were glorious times for him, and that the struggle of the Greeks was not unlike that of the Americans for freedom. He offered to aid the cause of Greece by donating 2,000 acres of land to which he was entitled by an act of the legislature of New York, passed in March, 1781. He said his labors in defending the frontiers of New York, by which he earned that bounty, were by far the most arduous of any that he performed during the whole revolutionary war; that there was more fatigue, more hazard and more anxiety in one of those campaigns than in seven such as he had served under Washington. Such is Col. Willett a testimony as to his labors in Tryon County.

In 1824, presidential electors in New York were appointed by the legislature; Col. Willett was one of the appointees, and was elected president of the Electoral College.

Whether he voted for John Quincy Adams, Gen. Jackson, Henry Clay or William H. Crawford, all of them candidates, I have not ascertained. In 1824, President Monroe, pursuant to a resolve of Congress invited Lafayette to become the guest of this nation; he accepted the invitation, but modestly declined the offer of a conveyance to this country in a United Slates ship of the line.

He left Havre July 12, 1824, and after a voyage of 34 days, arrived off Sandy Hook quite early in the morning of Sunday, August 15. Forty thousand people crowded the Battery to cheer and welcome his coming. Among the very first to meet and take Lafayette by the hand, was Joseph Bonaparte, then residing at Bordentown, New Jersey, ex-king of Spain, and brother of the great Napoleon.

At 9 O'clock in the morning, a small vessel steamed up to quarantine to take Lafayette direct to the city, but as it was Sunday and he was to have a public reception in New York on the morrow he declined to go, but, instead, went straightway to the residence of Vice President Daniel D. Tompkins on Staten Island. It was near forty years since Lafayette had left this country, and when his feet once again touched American soil, the memories of the past, the great changes since his first coming, came rushing to the front in the thoughts of the thronging multitude who witnessed his landing, and the emotions were too great for suppression too great to find utterance, except by salutes from all the ships in the harbor, the roaring of cannon, the ringing of bells and the loud acclaim of the people that the illustrious guest of the nation might receive a joyous and universal welcome.

Nothing like it had ever before been witnessed on this continent. In the afternoon a vessel steamed over to Staten

Island, taking a deputation from the common council of New York and a number of officers and soldiers of the revolutionary army, who had served under or with Lafayette. Among the number was Col. Willett.

Those two became acquainted in 1778, while with Washington in the Jerseys and at the battle of Monmouth on June 28 of that year. A correspondence had been kept up between them subsequent to the close of the war, and many of Lafayette s letters are now in possession of the youngest son of Col. Willett and are in an excellent state of preservation and show, in their perfect legibility and neatness, the care with which Lafayette's correspondence was always conducted. The English of the letters is faultless in construction and orthography. For the purpose of preservation, and as showing the strong friendship existing between those two soldiers, I herewith copy the whole of one letter and extracts from others:

PARIS, July 13, 1822.

My Dear Sir:

I avail myself of a good opportunity to remind you of your old friend and fellow-soldier in whose heart no time or distance can abate the patriotic remembrance and personal affections of our Revolutionary career. We remain but two survivors of that glorious epoch in which the fate of the two hemispheres has been decided. It is an additional reason to cherish more and more the ties of brotherly friendship which unite us. I find myself again engaged in a critical struggle between right and privilege.

May it be in my power before I join our departed companions to visit such of them as are still inhabitants of the United States and to tell you person ally my dear Willett, how affectionately I am

Your sincere friend

Lafayette.

Under date of July 1, 1824, a short time before Lafayette sailed from Europe he wrote Col. Willett in which he says: "The time most happy to me approaches when I shall embrace my old friend and brother soldiers", and concludes, "most truly and affectionately yours, Lafayette."

Under date of April 12, 1826, after his return to France, he writes: "Happy I am in every opportunity to renew and to form American connections. In so pleasing company I enjoy those feelings of American home which were never obliterated in my mind. Be pleased dear Willett, to let me hear from you and of the state of your health. Present my affectionate regards first in your house, then to your neighbors and to all our military companions and other friends in New York. Ever truly and affectionately your old friend and brother in arms, Lafayette".

Under date of April 6, 1828, he writes:

"My dear Willett: It is fit I should present to our senior revolutionary comrade a son of the illustrious and unfortunate Marshal Ney, who intends to visit the United States. I doubly rejoice in every opportunity to hear from you and to offer the best wishes and tender regards of your affectionate brother soldier, Lafayette."

Under date of Christmas, 1828, he writes again and concludes his letter as follows:

"Be pleased to remember me most affectionately to all our dear comrades in New York and vicinity and to your family knowing me to be forever.

Your affectionate friend and brother in arms,

LAFAYETTE.

Col. Willett."

The meeting between Lafayette and Col. Willett, at the house of Vice President Tompkins is described by an eye-witness as extremely affectionate and touching. They embraced and kissed each other over and over again, like devoted lovers, and Lafayette talking to Col. Willett very tenderly. The former was then sixty-seven years old, and Col. Willett eighty-four.

During the time Lafayette was in New York he was a frequent visitor at Col. Willett's residence, and the two were as much together as Lafayette could find time to spare from the receptions and ovations almost constantly awaiting him. On Friday, August 20th, the nation's guest left New York for Boston, in a coach drawn by four white horses accompanied by numerous delegations and escorted by the military. That same eye-witness, who describes that visit of Lafayette, says that the cavalcade which escorted him from the city, passed in its route fields of cabbages, and other agricultural products then growing upon the site now occupied by the Fifth Avenue Hotel. Those yet alive, whose memories go back sixty-five years, may remember Lafayette s tour through this valley in 1825.

The legislature of New York, by an act passed in October, 1779, attainted fifty-eight persons (three of whom were ladies) of treason, and confiscated their property. Among the number was John Tabor Kempe, the last Tory Attorney General of New York, and then the owner of one-sixteenth of Coxe's Patent, or tract of 47,000 acres, which stretches across what are now Rome, Westmoreland, Whitestown, Kirkland, New Hartford, Marshall, Paris and Bridgewater, in Oneida county. His wife before marriage was Grace Coxe, one of the patentees and also part owner of that patent. On a subdivision of that patent and a sale of Mr. Kempe's share under that confiscation act, George Washington, Governor George Clinton and Col. Willett became owners of land in the patent. Col. Willett became purchaser, in August, 1784, of over seven hundred acres, part of it not far from Hampton village in Westmoreland. Alex. Parkman, who moved into that town in 1790, obtained title to one hundred acres from Col. Willett.

The latter was also the owner of two thousand acres, known as "Willett's patent", in the north part of the town of Steuben, in this county, next to the Ava town line; he, with Elias

Van Benscoten, owned fifteen hundred acres in the town of Ava, next north of above two thousand acre tract, and called "Willett's small patent". Col. Willett also owned lands in Bayard s patent and in Twenty Township tract, Chenango County, hence, it is evident Oneida county people should be farther attracted and drawn toward one who was largely interested in lands in this county and vicinity so soon after the revolution, and fourteen years before Oneida county was organized.

Not long after the close of the revolutionary war, and probably within the last decade of the last century, Col. Willett purchased, for a homestead, a large parcel of vacant ground in what is now the thirteenth ward of New York city, near Corlear s Hook, extending from East River to what is now Willett street on the west. It is bounded northerly by DeLancey and southerly by Broome Street. It was then quite out of the city and far into the suburbs. A long range of hills loomed up between that purchase and Broadway, so that a sight of the then seeming busy city was shut out from the view, and a long space of vacant ground intervened and had to be traversed before schools, churches and the marts of trade were reached from that homestead. The land toward East River was shelving, so that the rushing waters made frequent inroads and gradual encroachments upon the lower portions, to obviate which the dirt from the range of hills in front was, in due time, moved to the rear of the lot next to the river, and in that way the waves were stayed and a fine water frontage created.

To improve and make that home pleasant and attractive, Col. Willett expended much money and labor, and many years of his life. The grounds were tastefully laid out into a garden, walks, carriageways and arbors, with fruit and shade trees planted upon and around the enclosure. A long row of poplars fringed the garden on one side, while cedar and other evergreens embellished or shaded the walks and other parts of the grounds. These trees were planted some years before the present century, for the eldest son alive of Col. Willett, now eighty-seven, writes me they were full grown at his earliest recollection.

Not far from the center of those grounds the owner built a large, commodious and roomy dwelling, and there, for over a quarter of a century, he entertained his numerous visitors and callers, with a welcome and a generous hospitality, that no one knows better, if so well, how to extend, than an army officer who has seen much of the world; there too, he furnished a home and a cordial welcome to dependent relatives, to whom he was all that the most kind and indulgent parent could be. Although not a millionaire, yet he was in comfortable circumstances, kept his horses and carriage, lived generously for those times, all of which could be done in those days of frugality and simplicity, on an income of five or six thousand dollars a year.

One day last summer that eldest son crossed over from Jersey City to revisit the scenes of his childhood, that he might give a better description for this paper prepared in memory of his father, of that old homestead and of the grounds where his feet rambled when a boy. But indeed how changed; seven or eight busy streets now cross those grounds, while the site of the garden, the walks, the carriage-ways, the trees, the arbors, is now occupied by solid brick structures like Hoe's Printing Press Works, large Catholic Church, and buildings of that description; yet in his mind's eye he again saw the home as it was early in the present century, the long range of hills, over which he climbed on his way to school, the playground, the boys of his youth, the fruit trees which yielded profusely, the large favorite cherry tree, capable of holding a small army of boys upon its huge and wide spreading branches, stood out a conspicuous figure as he looked back over the vista of years; many an afternoon in summer at the close of school, a hundred boys could be found ensconced in that generons tree, partaking of its seeming inexhaustible supply, with a zest and a relish that no one can enjoy so well as a schoolboy. He of all others, in that great city, was probably the only survivor who could remember, in all its details, those grounds as they were years ago. During Col. Willett s residence there and for years thereafter that old homestead was widely known as "Cedar Grove" or "The Willett Place".

In 1783, Col. Willett was among the active persons who formed the Society of Cincinnati, having for its object the promotion of brotherly feeling among the officers who served in the war of the revolution. When Lafayette visited this country in 1824, he was the only surviving major general who belonged to that society, so too, Col. Willett was a member of the Tammany society, formed about the same time, more for the purpose, however, of keeping in check the apprehended tendency of the government to monarchy; not until many years later, did it become an organization to promote the success of a political party.

Col. Willett was three times married. The first marriage was to Mary Pease in April, 1760, before he was quite twenty years of age. By that marriage one son was born, who became a noted surgeon in the United States army, and who died unmarried.

Unto the second marriage no children were born. The third wife was Margaretta Bancker, married not far from 1800; by her he had four children. The eldest son, Marinus, was a physician, and married and had children; he is now deceased. William M. was the second son by that marriage; married and now eighty-seven years old, and living in Jersey City, a retired divine of the Methodist Episcopal Church; was a member of the Methodist Episcopal General Conference in 1826; later, an instructor in Hebrew and Biblical literature in Wesleyan University and editor.

In 1843 he founded the Biblical Institute in Vermont, of which he was president until 1848. Edward, the other son, is a lawyer by profession, now eighty-six years old, and residing at Brook Green, S. C. The fourth child was Margaretta, who married

James H. Ray and died years ago. The widow of Col. Willett died in 1867, at the age of ninety-six.

Col. Willett was tall, erect, commanding figure, finely proportioned, with the air and build of a military man. His face was handsome, his eyes blue, his countenance very pleasing and attractive, and his manners those of a courteous and cultivated gentleman. One of his full length portraits, taken when he was thirty-five years old, in continental uniform, by Trumbull, is now in possession of his youngest son, as are the sword and hanger worn by Col. Willett during the war. A portrait of Col. Willett is shown on page 272 of Lossing's History of the Empire State.

Col. Willett was a plain, blunt man, outspoken, perfectly fearless, & hater of all shams and an enthusiastic patriot. His acquaintance and correspondence with the prominent men of his day were extensive. His son has dozens of letters to his father from Governor Clinton, Aaron Burr, Lafayette, Lord Stirling, and men of like character. He and Burr were in early times intimate friends, but after the duel with Hamilton, and Burr's trial for treason, they lived to meet and pass each other on the street without recognition.

Col. Willett admired the political writings of Thomas Paine, but after the publication of "Paine s Age of Reason", his works were altogether discarded by Willett. He was a faithful attendant at the Protestant Episcopal Church, (St. Stephen's), then located on Christie Street, one block from the Bowery, and about a mile from Col. Willett s residence.

In a foot note in Lossing's Empire State it is stated Col. Willett graduated from King's, now Columbia College. This may admit of some doubt, when it is remembered that Col. Willett entered the army before he was eighteen, and married before he was twenty. Nevertheless he was a person of unusually strong mind, strengthened by observation and extensive reading. His correspondence and official army reports are clear and marked with accuracy and precision. As a public speaker he was a model.

The fact that Col. Gansevoort deputed him to reply to St. Leger's demand for the surrender of Fort Stanwix, indicates that his ability in that line was recognized by the commanding officer.

That speech deserves a place in every history and rhetorical school book in the land, alongside of Patrick Henry's "Give me liberty, or give me death".

Among the last public acts of Col. Willett were, in 1824, while acting as chairman of the Greek committee, presidential elector, and welcoming Lafayette. During the last few years of his life he mingled but little in public affairs and with the outside world; surrounded by his family and immediate friends, he yielded slowly, but not reluctantly, to the gradual progress of decay.

He had outlived his generation, and passed his fourscore years; his mind was constantly fixed upon the approaching change with trust and entire resignation; with the greatest humility, but at the same time with the liveliest feelings of piety. A few months before his death he was attacked with paralysis, from which he recovered; yet his body and constitution were much enfeebled by the stroke; medicine had to be frequently resorted to the absence of his regular physician, in one of his attacks, induced him to neglect the usual remedies, and he was so severely attacked that his strength wasted rapidly away.

On Sunday, August 22, 1830, the fifty-third anniversary of the abandonment of the siege of Fort Stanwix, Col. Willett passed peacefully away twenty-two days past his ninetieth birthday.

It is related, that as the shadows of death were curtaining the earthly vision of Stonewall Jackson, he, in the delirium of his dying, was again in the roar of battle, and amid the clangor of arms, and called out "Order A. P. Hill to prepare for action. Pass the infantry to the front rapidly. Tell Major Hawkes" then he stopped, leaving the sentence unfinished. Presently a smile of in effable sweetness spread itself over his wan face, "as if his soul had seen a vision,"; and then he said calmly and quietly, "let us cross over the river, and rest under the shade of the trees", then without pain or a struggle, his spirit passed peacefully away.

Col. Willett had been amid scenes of carnage and bloodshed; he had lived in turbulent times, and been exposed to innumerable perils; he had braved dangers, faced death, escaped the hissing bullet, the poisoned arrow, the glittering tomahawk, and the murderous scalping knife, and survived to the grand old age of 90, to receive the homage and plaudits of a grateful people, and to die at last surrounded by his family and friends.

He too, crossed over the river, and rested* under the shade of the trees. His death cast a deep gloom over the whole city, and called forth deep and heart felt expressions of sorrow. The Common Council of New York, the Court of Errors, then in session in that city, the society of Cincinnati, and other public bodies passed suitable resolutions, and resolved to attend his funeral in a body. The military of the city directed that appropriate honors should be paid at the interment, and that minute guns should be fired, corresponding with his age.

The public journals of the day, not in New York alone, but throughout the country, paid handsome and well-deserved tributes to his memory. The remains were enclosed in a cedar coffin, which the deceased had prepared ten years before; at his own request the body was habitated in his ordinary dress and with his hat on, as he was accustomed to be seen in the street.

The coffined remains were placed in an arbor upon the grounds of the old homestead on the day of the funeral, that all who chose might take a farewell look.

It was estimated that over ten thousand persons availed themselves of the opportunity. The funeral took place in the afternoon of Tuesday, August 24, at which officiated Rev. Dr. DeWitt, a son of an old officer of the revolution under Col. Willett. The procession started at 4 p. M. for the place of burial, and it extended from Broome street to Trinity Church yard, where the remains were to be interred. It was after dark before the grave was reached and by the light of torches all that was earthly of Col. Marinus Willett was lowered to his last resting place amid the firing of guns, the strains of martial music and the sorrows of millions of his admiring countrymen.

Other heroes of the revolution may stand out more prominently on the pages of recorded history; other names may be perpetuated in poetry and song, in flowing numbers and in brighter colors; other men may be kept alive in the world's remembrance by lettered inscriptions of their heroic deeds emblazoned upon chiseled marble or sculptured monuments, but none who lived in the trying and troublous times of Col. Willett more faithfully or efficiently than he, and certainly none within the county of Tryon, performed the important work assigned to him, which in the result worked out the grand problem of his country's destiny. He was a fearless leader, an enthusiastic patriot, a worthy citizen and an uncompromising friend of the rights of man.

Made in the USA
Middletown, DE
12 November 2014